SPEAKING OUT FOR PSYCHIATRY
A Handbook for Involvement with the Mass Media

Report No. 124

SPEAKING OUT FOR PSYCHIATRY

A Handbook for Involvement with the Mass Media

Formulated by the
Committee on Public Education

Group for the Advancement of Psychiatry

BRUNNER/MAZEL *Publishers* • New York

Library of Congress Cataloging-in-Publication Data

Group for the Advancement of Psychiatry. Committee on
Public Education.
Speaking out for psychiatry.

(Report; no. 124)
Includes bibliographies.
1. Mass media in mental health education. 2. Psychiatry.
I. Title. II. Series: Report (Group for the Advancement of
Psychiatry); no. 124.
[DNLM: 1. Health Education—handbooks. 2. Mass Media
—handbooks. 3. Mental Health—handbooks. 4. Psychiatry
—handbooks. W1 RE209BR no. 124 / WM 34 G882s]
RC321.G7 no. 124 [RA790.87] 616.89 s 87-24229
ISBN 0-87630-488-9 [616.89'00141]
ISBN 0-87630-487-0 (pbk.)

Published by
BRUNNER/MAZEL, INC.
19 Union Square West
New York, New York 10003

MANUFACTURED IN THE UNITED STATES OF AMERICA

10 9 8 7 6 5 4 3 2 1

STATEMENT OF PURPOSE

THE GROUP FOR THE ADVANCEMENT OF PSYCHIATRY has a membership of approximately 300 psychiatrists, most of whom are organized in the form of a number of working committees. These committees direct their efforts toward the study of various aspects of psychiatry and the application of this knowledge to the fields of mental health and human relations.

Collaboration with specialists in other disciplines has been and is one of GAP's working principles. Since the formation of GAP in 1946, its members have worked closely with such other specialists as anthropologists, biologists, economists, statisticians, educators, lawyers, nurses, psychologists, sociologists, social workers, and experts in mass communication, philosophy, and semantics. GAP envisages a continuing program of work according to the following aims:

1. To collect and appraise significant data in the fields of psychiatry, mental health, and human relations;
2. To reevaluate old concepts and to develop and test new ones;
3. To apply the knowledge thus obtained for the promotion of mental health and good human relations.

GAP is an independent group, and its reports represent the composite findings and opinions of its members only, guided by its many consultants.

Speaking Out for Psychiatry: A Handbook for Involvement with the Mass Media was formulated by the Committee on Public Education. The members of this committee are listed on page vii. The members of the other GAP committees, as well as additional membership categories and current and past officers of GAP, are listed on pp. 000–000.

Committee on Public Education
Group for the Advancement of Psychiatry

Robert A. Solow, M.D., *Chairman*

Susan J. Blumenthal, M.D.
Robert J. Campbell, M.D.
Keith H. Johansen, M.D.
Steven E. Katz, M.D.
Norman L. Loux, M.D.
Harvey L. Ruben, M.D.
Julius Schreiber, M.D.
Kenneth N. Vogtsberger, M.D.

Elise H. Richman, M.D., *Fellow*
Calvin R. Summer, M.D., *Fellow*
Lucy Freeman, *Ittleson Consultant*

CONTENTS

---

*Reprinted with the permission and courtesy of the Division of Public Affairs and the Joint Commission on Public Affairs of the American Psychiatric Association.

SPEAKING OUT FOR PSYCHIATRY

A Handbook for Involvement with the Mass Media

INTRODUCTION

The future of psychiatry may well depend on our ability to educate the public effectively. The past two decades have seen periods of rapid change in the health care field. An informed public needs to be aware of current concepts in mental health and the unique distinctions between providers. Psychiatry must endorse the concept of public education as an essential activity of the field. The mass media are the most powerful means of reaching the public, delivering new information, and shaping public attitudes. Effective public education depends on developing psychiatry's relationship with the media. This will allow psychiatry to utilize the power of the print and electronic media productively in reaching the general public.

Traditionally, the attitude of many psychiatrists with regard to the media has been, "No news is good news!" The often negative and inaccurately stereotyped depiction of psychiatrists in the media has contributed to this attitude. But, psychiatry should accept some responsibility for the persistent misrepresentations of the field in order to develop a more effective collaboration. Psychiatrists have often been unavailable to and uncooperative with the media, anticipating every encounter as adversarial. Ignorance of the communication professions has led to miscommunications. Many psychiatrists are unskilled in translating the principles and practice of the field into terms understandable by the media and their audience.

The media response to these difficulties has been to turn for information to other mental health practitioners who have been more available, cooperative and communicative. Those willing to work with the media have come to be regarded as "experts" by the public, irrespective of their actual expertise. Psychiatry has been devalued relative to the more media-cooperative mental health professions, if for no other reason than deficient exposure. The general public has little alternative but to accept as valid the portrayal of psychiatry in parody and caricature.

Only public education can begin to overcome the negative image that some of the public hold about psychiatry and the myths they harbor about mental illness. Only through education can the public recognize the necessity for including mental illness in comprehensive health insurance programs.

This handbook addresses how psychiatrists can most effectively be involved in public education and thus combat destructive attitudes. It discusses the various forms of the mass media and the part they play in molding public policy. It looks at some of psychiatry's reluctance in the past to take full advantage of the opportunities the media offer to educate the public. It provides a guide to some of the practical problems that may be encountered in working with the media. It also discusses some of the ethical issues involved and some of the implications of an interaction between psychiatry and the media.

This handbook is neither an introduction to the theory of communications, nor an instructional manual on becoming a television personality or a feature writer for a major daily. Instead, it draws on the expertise of its authors to provide a guide to the most common situations a psychiatrist is likely to encounter, with suggestions on how to prepare for them and how to handle them.

The Power of the Media

Surveys indicate that most Americans get their first news in the morning from the radio. Many Americans watch hours of television daily. Billions of magazine copies are purchased a year, frequently to be read, reread, and shared. Newspapers are ubiquitous. The mass media, like all forms of communication, are designed to inform, influence and persuade. They do so on a grand scale.

No one questions the impact television, radio and print have on

American thinking. Many times, however, the views presented are distorted. Intended distortions usually serve the function of promoting controversy. The need to capture the interest of an audience is served by being provocative and creating conflict. Availability to huge audiences is necessary but may not be sufficient to affect public opinion.

Professionals in the communications field appreciate the many factors that determine whether they will be successful. The audience, the message, the source of the information, and the type of medium used to express it are critical variables. Not unlike psychiatrists, competent editors are aware of their own attitudes toward their audience and the messages they deliver. They must believe in what they are doing to be effective. Editors also understand the needs, the strengths, and the weaknesses of their chosen medium. They sense whether and how they can effectively communicate given material. Finally, they accurately perceive their audience. What are their communication behaviors? What do they read, listen to, watch? What is their rationale for "tuning in" this medium? What is their attitude toward the medium? For any given subject, editors are sensitive to the knowledge of their audience and their attitudes toward both the subject and the source of information. To the extent that editors, consciously or unconsciously, take these factors into account, they are effective. Their audience accepts and is influenced by the view they communicate.

As psychiatrists, we can harness this power in order to teach the public about mental health, mental illness, and the role of psychiatry. To succeed, we must address the same factors as the editors. Who compose our audience? What are their attitudes and their communication behaviors? What message are we trying to transmit? What would be the most effective medium for reaching a given audience with a given message? What are our own attitudes toward those we wish to influence? Do we really believe in what we have to offer?

Psychiatrists are accustomed to soul-searching. We can grapple unassisted with the questions pertaining to ourselves and our message. However, we need to learn more about media and audiences. The best teacher is experience; most of us have little. The next best teacher is the experienced. Many professionals in the communications fields are glad to help us use their medium effectively, but we must be aware of and considerate of their particular needs.

Some understanding of how television, radio, newspaper and magazines operate will be provided in chapter six. There are some significant differences among them. Nonetheless, they are alike in an essential feature: They are all business enterprises. Whatever other functions they may serve, they need to make money to survive. To make money they must attract and satisfy both audiences and advertisers. When we deal with media representatives we should appreciate that they are pressured by deadlines, policies, and perhaps politics. More importantly, we should remember that they represent a business. As in any business, their product must be marketable and competitive. Accordingly, we can, without compromising our standards or waiving our professional authority or sacrificing our dignity, adapt to their functional needs, and they can help fulfill ours.

1

WHO'S WATCHING, LISTENING AND READING?

Seldom does a week go by on the *Today Show, Good Morning America,* or the *CBS Morning News* without a feature report concerning a topic of mental health interest. Even the evening news shows often report on topics pertaining to mental health or mental illness. Subjects such as eating disorders, depression, teenage suicide, the effects of divorce on children, alcoholism, and drug abuse are frequent fare in television news. Interest is also reflected in the plethora of mental health call-in shows carried on both national and local radio.

In a recent hour on a nationally broadcast radio call-in show, hosted by a psychiatrist, the following eight persons called: 1) A grandmother complained that her adult children were allowing the family dog to lick their 16-month-old child on the face. She wondered whether her daughter was "crazy." 2) A 70-year-old widow of four years missed her husband and was concerned about how to meet a man. 3) A 63-year-old man was being treated for depression with two antidepressants and was concerned about vivid dreams he had experienced. 4) A woman's 17-year-old son, after one and one-half years in therapy with a psychologist, continued to be depressed and very hostile. She was wondering whether a different form of therapy would be more appropriate. 5) A 24-year-old woman's best friend (a recent college graduate, married, with a child) was just killed in an automobile accident. The caller was in a state of shock and asking for help in dealing with it. 6) A 37-year-old woman asked for help dealing with the termination of a long-sustained relationship. 7) A 20-year-old suicidal college student had been experiencing thoughts of dying for three to four years and was concerned about how to obtain appropriate help. 8) A 40-year-old divorcee, who had been in a series of relationships with abusive men, was upset when her therapist told her that she was actually seeking out such men. She wanted to know whether it could be true.

Why did they call? Why had they not sought advice from their family doctor or gone to a community mental health resource in their own area and sought help in person? There are a number of possible answers. It becomes clear from listening to call-in shows that many people do not know where else to turn. They do not know whether or how to approach the mental health system. Many have no family doctor, and they can think of no other alternative. They call seeking advice, much as one might go to an emergency room or primary care center seeking immediate attention for a physical problem. Some have ventured into the mental health treatment system, but with only limited benefit, and are looking for alternative routes to follow in their quest for help. Some who are in treatment may not like the advice of their own therapists and, therefore, call seeking a second opinion. Finally, a number may have been listening to the host for a relatively long period of time and, having acquired a sense of trust in him, call when a problem of their own occurs. The host is the first person to whom they think of turning.

Why are these call-in shows and these news reports so well received? The answer rests in part with the fact that almost everyone is affected to some extent by emotional upset and/or emotional illness. The Mid-Town Manhattan study, which was carried out at Columbia University in the early 1950s (Srole et al., 1962), revealed that in a large population of people studied in New York City, over 80 percent had experienced *symptoms* which would have been amenable to psychiatric treatment at some point in their lives. The recently reported Epidemiological Catchment Area Survey, carried out by the National Institutes of Mental Health over the last several years in five major cities (Regier et al., 1984), revealed that 20 percent of the people in the United States are suffering from some *diagnosable* psychiatric illness. What's more, only one-fifth of these are receiving any kind of treatment. Given that situation, almost everyone has either experienced emotional symptoms or illness themselves or witnessed it in family members or friends. Thus, there is a great hunger for information about the nature, the course, and the treatment of various problems. That the caller is not face to face with the host and no fee is involved are also factors to be considered.

A large segment of the American population does spend a considerable amount of time watching and listening to television and radio. According to the A.C. Nielsen Company report of October 1984, the average American viewer watched 28.46 hours of television per week. Women 18–34 years of age watched 39.48 hours; 35–54 years, 30.22 hours; and over 55 years, 40.14 hours. Men watched less television throughout their lives until 55, from which time they watched 35.49 hours (Traub, 1985). The GAP report, *The Child and Television Drama* (1982), notes that by age 18, a typical teenager will have spent one and one-half to two times as many hours in front of a television set as in school. These figures are staggering. People do not realize how much time they spend in front of the television set. Background radio is ubiquitous in the modern American home and car. The average listener phases in and out, attending to some parts of the program and not to others. Issues pertaining to mental health and mental illness seem to garner listening attention more frequently than other topics.

A debate has arisen within the media and within the mental health profession as to whether or not the mental health call-in shows and news reports are entertainment or education. The fact that the shows attract such large audiences allows them to obtain commercial sponsorship without difficulty. Commercial sponsors have traditionally used entertainment as a way to showcase their products. However, those who tune in regularly say that the shows do more to educate than to entertain. These shows generate a large amount of mail, and writers frequently comment on the educational value of the programming. Another frequent comment is that hearing how others solve their problems, helps the listeners or viewers to determine how to approach their own.

What is the power of the media? Is it illusory or does it really exist? The response to these questions is a resounding affirmation of the media's true influence on viewers, listeners and readers. A recent comment by Ann Landers stating that a pamphlet on depression was available from the National Institutes of Mental Health brought forth thousands of requests. Dear Abby received a similar response to a comment concerning the difficulties of caring for a psychotic person at home, which led to a recently published GAP report (1986) on the subject. The Washington Psychiatric Society ran a public service announcement on a local television station giving information about depression and received several thousand requests for referrals on a hot-line phone number they made available. An announcement on a mental health issues call-in show that the Cornell Medical School Affective Disorders Clinic was offering free treatment brought a deluge of responses, which continued for several months.

Behavioral scientists have conducted systematic studies of the media's influence. McAbee and Cafferty (1982) pointed out the ability of television and radio to notify potential patients quickly of the availability of services. Focusing attention on a geriatric population, they placed public service announcements on local television stations and found a marked increase in the number of calls requesting information and services. They pointed out that it was possible to use the media not as a "mass communication, but as a targeted communication."

Similarly, Schanie and Sundel (1978) engaged the mass media in a prevention project in Louisville, Kentucky. They aired 21 public service announcements on radio and television for six weeks, focusing on themes relating to mental health or mental retardation. They found that the public awareness of community mental health agencies was nearly doubled during the course of that project. In Finland, McAlister, Puska, Koskela, Pallonen and Maccoby (1980) devised a nationwide month-long television program and followed up with a one-month publicity campaign encouraging people to stop smoking. They found that one percent of those surveyed nationally had ceased smoking and had maintained cessation for at least six months. The cost of the program was approximately one dollar per six months of success per person.

Munoz and his colleagues (1982) used the local San Francisco TV news to broadcast short messages about cognitive-behavioral prevention for depression. The project was evaluated before and after airing to determine short-term effects. The data collected included subjective evaluations of the message, behavioral techniques used by the viewers, information about the specific messages, and depression levels. The majority of random viewers contacted felt that the messages were clear and practical. They had been persuaded to use several of the suggested techniques to help themselves. People who had experienced depression before the airing reported a decrease in their depression after watching the series. Although the study was designed as a primary prevention effort, it actually brought individuals into treatment in a form of secondary prevention.

Considering the foregoing, it is clear that the media can and does exert a major effect on those who watch, listen, and read. This should be considered when devising any type of community-wide educational program. To consider a show about mental health issues merely as entertainment would be a gross underestimation of its overall effect.

Looking at radio call-in shows, one researcher (Rubenstein, 1981) studying loneliness by questionnaire found that two percent of 4,900 respondents had called talk shows regarding personal problems. Following up specifically on that two percent, the researcher reported that they appeared not to be isolated from their world, but instead seemed well tied into their own social support system. What seemed to distinguish them was willingness to publicize their problems. Almost 75 percent of the callers had already discussed their problem with friends or relatives; about half the callers were or had been engaged in some form of therapy; more than half had called several other radio shows. Most callers evidently were not displeased with the brief format of radio, expecting perhaps an alternative point of view, or just an understanding ally. Many callers manifested a superficial view of psychology and psychiatry in general—"It's something that exists to solve people's mental problems." The author concluded that the greatest good from mental health programs might be realized by the 98 percent of listeners who do not call. For them, it may provide an "electronic support network." In fact, those who call often praise the show for the tremendous support they have felt as listeners in the past.

In another study (Colford, 1985), 122 callers to a mental health talk show were interviewed, first while their calls were on hold, and again after the broadcast. While the majority found the experience to be helpful, 64 percent of the callers commented that they would have liked their on-air experience to last longer. In Chapter 3, we will take an in-depth look at a radio call-in show as a case illustration.

Although a systematic study of the type and number of mental health shows in the media has yet to be done, it is obvious that such shows are influential and popular. Their number increases yearly. An Association for Media Psychology was founded in 1982, indicating the increasing attention being paid to this area of mental health practice. Its vast influence cannot be denied. Let us hope that soon we, as a profession, will have learned how to add the media effectively to our therapeutic armamentarium.

2

WHY BOTHER?

Maximizing the media's coverage of psychiatric issues and the psychiatric profession presents a vital challenge for our field. Granted, involvement in public affairs represents a striking departure from the customary activity of most psychiatrists. We find efforts at image building unfamiliar and difficult, and many psychiatrists will ask, "Why bother?" There are several important reasons.

Educating the Public about Mental Illness

Most Americans still do not understand what mental illness is. They think of a mental disorder as a weakness or sin rather than as an illness that is treatable. They do not clearly differentiate between mental illness and mental retardation, nor can they explain psychotherapy or how it works. The general public does not totally understand that treatment of mental disorders can reduce demand for other kinds of health care as well as the overall cost of health care. In addition, the public lacks full awareness of the value of psychiatric services and the knowledge that psychiatric practices are based on an increasing body of valid scientific medical research.

Stereotypes about psychiatrists and myths about mental illness can be corrected by working with the mass media. This means working with both local and national media and becoming visible in local communities. It means presenting scientific evidence and explaining how it is translated into clinical practice. If psychiatrists help people understand that mental disorders are illnesses, help remove the stigma of mental illness, and inform people about treatment and its effectiveness and where to go for help, they can hope to alter the public perception of their profession as well as to aid the mentally ill and lessen the enormous tax strain caused by mental illness.

Advocating for the Patient

Psychiatrists should use the media to advocate for those suffering from mental illness. A significant proportion of the homeless, for example, through mental illness and/or substance abuse, are unable to speak for themselves. The importance of increasing financial support of prophylactic psychiatric services should be emphasized. Problems such as the public financing of state mental institutions need to be addressed. So, too, the public ought to understand DRGs and PPOs in terms of maximizing patient benefits in the midst of an economic revolution in the practice of medicine. Psychiatrists also need to work with patients and their families to build support for psychiatric services. For example, they can form ties with organizations such as the National Alliance for the Mentally Ill and the Mental Health Association. By news interviews and appearances on talk shows, psychiatrists can inform the public about such specific mental health issues.

Disseminating Information about the Cost to Society of Mental Illness

Improved media relations would help psychiatrists communicate information about a number of issues that affect the practice of psychiatry and the public welfare. Taking the time to talk to members of the media would make the public and other health care providers more knowledgeable about what services exist for treating mental disorders. In addition, it would illuminate inequities in the financing of mental health compared to other health care services.

Reinforcing the Availability of Mental Health Services

One American in five is estimated to be suffering from a mental disorder. Many of these people do not seek treatment. Often they do not know where to turn for help. Many see a health care professional who does not properly diagnose their disorder or prescribe the appropriate treatment. Psychiatrists, working through the media, can increase public awareness of the signs and symptoms of mental disorders, the kinds of treatments available, and where help can be found. Available mental health services include partial or part-time hospitalization, 24-hour residential treatment, emergency and crisis intervention, consultation-liaison, social support, and outpatient psychotherapy.

Psychiatrists can enlighten the public about the reasons for and the disastrous results of the deinstitutionalization movement and the fact that most psychiatric disorders can be treated on an outpatient basis. People need to become aware that there are thousands of chronically mentally ill patients who are homeless and on the streets and who need treatment. Unfortunately, communities have not supplied enough community-based alternative services, even though ambulatory psychiatric services have increased over the past several decades. By 1977, they accounted for 72 percent of all psychiatric care encounters.

Clarifying the Psychiatrist's Role

The general public has a limited perception of what various mental health specialists actually do. Even the media sometimes manifest difficulty distinguishing among psychiatrists, psychologists, and social workers. When reporters and commentators are preparing a story, they might well profit from the clarification of professional psychiatric opinion in their presentation. Psychiatrists have generally been more reluctant than psychologists to talk to the media. Their reluctance allows other mental health professionals to step in and serves to blur the distinctions between the two fields.

It is clearly to psychiatrists' advantage to become involved with the media so they can educate the media and the public about psychiatrists' special skills in diagnosing and treating mental disorders. Psychiatrists can clarify their own distinctive role if they let the media and public know wherein their special training, skills and functions differ from other mental health professionals.

As a growing number of mental health specialists and other physicians become eligible for third party reimbursement and the competition for patients increases, it becomes vital for the public to understand the role of the psychiatrist. The media provide an opportunity to educate the public to the fact that psychiatrists are physicians with special skills in the diagnosis and treatment of mental disorders.

Improving the Image of the Psychiatrist

Acquiring a positive public image is critical for psychiatrists today. The bad press that psychiatrists have received, the public's ignorance of what psychiatrists do, and increasing services by other mental health specialists are factors that necessitate psychiatrists paying greater attention to the media. Working with the media can enable psychiatrists to promote a more positive image of the profession, to instruct laymen about mental health issues, and to demystify psychiatry. More familiarizing efforts are needed like that of the American Psychiatric Association's Division of Public Affairs, which has helped to train psychiatrists to understand and work with the media.

In summary, in appropriate media relations there are many potential benefits for the psychiatric profession and the public. The media can enhance the psychiatrist's image and role in the community, improve the conceptualization by the public and other health care providers about mental illnesses and their treatment, raise public awareness of inequities that plague the funding of mental health services, and diminish the stigma of mental illness. All these factors can serve to relieve suffering and decrease the costs of mental illness to society.

3

A CASE IN POINT: A RADIO MENTAL HEALTH CALL-IN SHOW

A member of the GAP Public Education Committee (Ruben, 1986) has hosted a national mental health issues radio call-in show for over four years. The three-hour show is featured every Saturday and Sunday night on over 290 stations in 50 states, and reaches close to 5 million listeners. During an average hour the host answers 8 to 10 calls. This means that each three-hour show handles about 27 calls, a total of approximately 2,500 calls a year.

Of the total calls, about 50 percent concern relationships with spouses, friends, parents or children; 25 percent want to learn about anxiety and depression; 15 percent concern eating disorders (including obesity), Alzheimer's disease, schizophrenia, manic-depressive illness, and borderline and sociopathic personality disorders. The remaining 10 percent inquire about such matters as sexual problems, different types of therapy, how to go about seeing a psychiatrist, how to deal with a troublesome boss or neighbor, or how to find a new job. In addition, over 100 people each week write letters asking for such information as a referral for the name of a drug mentioned on the air or the name of a self-help organization. About 25 percent give detailed information and request specific advice.

Who calls and who listens? The program coordinator screens and keeps a log of all the calls. Callers range in age from preadolescents to octogenarians. Approximately 40 percent of these are 25 to 45 years old; 20 percent, 18 to 25; 10 percent, under 18; 20 percent, 45 to 60; and 10 percent are over 60. Of the 100 calls screened each hour, about 20 are placed on hold to await getting on the air. Callers include students from grade school through graduate school, medical students and residents, housewives, businessmen, doctors, lawyers and engineers, night shift workers such as nurses, police, firefighters and security guards. A general practitioner in a small town, who was depressed, called because she had nowhere else to turn. Recently, individuals with cellular mobile phones in their cars have been calling. Interestingly, about 10 percent of the callers are visually impaired.

Half of the callers want information about a condition or situation. The rest request help or specific advice regarding a problem. Many want a second opinion as a check of their own therapist. Many realize that they need help but resist seeking it; they need to be told not only that they need it, but how and where to get it.

The screening of callers is a critically important function. On this particular show, screening is carried out by the program coordinator, who has extensive background in radio but no mental health training. No one is screened out who can clearly state a relevant problem that has not already been discussed in that particular hour. Severely upset or disturbed callers are handled by the host off-air during commercials and given an appropriate referral. Callers whose problem has already been discussed during that hour are asked to call back at another time. Those unable to articulate their problem clearly enough to be understood on the air are told there is a problem with their telephone line and asked to write their question in a letter to the host.

The host must instruct the large silent audience of listeners as well as the caller. The difference between psychiatrists and psychologists, and when to consult each, is usually explained once during each show. Listeners are helped to understand psychiatry and psychiatrists—what psychiatrists can or cannot do and when it is appropriate to turn to one for help. Callers are also referred to self-help resources such as the local mental health association, when appropriate. A vitally important service that the host performs is helping parents to understand that various behavioral approaches to child discipline, which are discussed on the program, are far more effective than physical coercion. It is emphasized that help is available for everyone, rich or poor. Referrals for professional treatment are made to mental health centers, psychiatric clinics, or to the local district branch of the American Psychiatric Association to obtain the names of qualified psychiatrists. A caller unacquainted with available resources in his/her area is referred to the state or local department of mental health in order to locate the nearest mental health facility. Callers are urged to seek advice in person so that they can obtain a complete evaluation of their problem.

On those occasions when it sounds as if a caller were being mismanaged or as though a therapist were behaving inappropriately, the caller is urged to seek a second opinion and, if deemed necessary, to contact the ethics committee of the appropriate local professional society to request an investigation.

The calls are, for the most part, interesting, compelling, and, at times, unique. Since calls come from all 50 states, one hears a diversity of situations rarely encountered in a private office.

> One woman, following a blow to her head, complained of headaches and dizziness. It was suggested that she might have a concussion, and she was directed to go to the nearest hospital emergency room. The following week, a nurse called to say that several days after that woman spoke to the host, she had stumbled into their emergency room mumbling that the talk show host had sent her. A neurosurgeon saw the patient and rushed her to surgery to evacuate a subdural hematoma.

> An 11-year-old girl called saying that her parents, in the process of getting a divorce, were fighting incessantly. She was an only child with no aunts or uncles or living grandparents. She said her parents had placed her in the middle, with each one telling her how the other one was bad, harmful and not concerned about her interests. She stated that she had no one to talk to and, therefore, had turned to the host. After exploring all possible avenues with him, she agreed to contact her minister with the hope that he would be able to bring the parents together and persuade them to stop using the child as a pawn in their marital discord.

An outspoken critic of psychiatry, who had been involved nationally with antipsychiatry activities, called and asked to speak to the host off the air. It appeared that she was suicidally depressed. She had locked herself in her room with a gun for four days. Since she was antipsychiatry, she felt she could not turn to anybody in her own area. The host discussed alternatives for seeking help with her. She ultimately agreed to see her family physician and ask him to treat her.

A 64-year-old widow, after 35 years of marriage, whose husband had died four months earlier of cancer, called to say that she was very upset and not able to cope. She was feeling helpless, hopeless and worthless. Her sleep was disturbed and she had lost her appetite. She had gone to two different psychiatrists. Each had tried to treat her with antidepressants, but she had experienced adverse reactions, including an allergic rash. She had stopped the medicine and was afraid to return to either psychiatrist because she feared that she would be placed on more medication. The host discussed with her the difference between normal grieving and a major depressive disorder. He suggested that although it seemed appropriate that the psychiatrists had attempted to treat her with antidepressants, it was also possible to treat her grief and depression with psychotherapy alone. He directed her to return to the psychiatrist with whom she felt most comfortable and ask to be treated solely with psychotherapy, given her fears of further medication.

A 42-year-old married woman called to explain that a referral by the host to Overeaters Anonymous over a year and a half earlier had led her to lose 50 pounds and achieve her normal weight. However, since that time, she had become promiscuous and involved in a number of sexual relationships without her husband's knowledge. She called because she was concerned about her behavior. Although part of her seemed to be enjoying it, she did not wish to continue the pattern, and she wanted to know how to seek help. She agreed to accept a referral for psychotherapy at the psychiatric outpatient department of a nearby medical school.

On the air, the host refers at least 75 percent of the callers for evaluation and treatment. The remaining 25 percent of the callers receive some advice—how to find a nursing home for a parent, how to deal with a child's misbehavior, or how to use self-help resources such as an organization or, perhaps, a book on relaxation techniques.

The host adheres strictly to the APA *Guidelines for the Psychiatrist Working with the Communications Media* (Joint Commission, 1977) (see Appendix 1). Explicit in the APA Guidelines is that a psychiatrist must not exploit anyone for the purpose of the media. It might make compelling radio fare to put an acutely suicidal person on the air, but that would be exploitation. It is the professional, ethical and moral responsibility of any psychiatrist functioning within arenas of the media to ensure that problem-stressed participants are helped, not exploited.

It is clear that people have valid and legitimate reasons to call. Few merely want to hear themselves on the radio. Either they are suffering from an emotional problem themselves, or they are concerned about emotional problems of their friends or relatives. They truly do not know where to turn. The vast, silently listening audience is able to identify with the callers. They hear others discuss situations like their own and gain solace from learning that they are not alone. Listeners are provided information that can help them determine some new coping styles and thereby help relieve their own problems. There is clearly a large, heretofore unmet need for input of this type into people's emotional functioning. The fact that 80 percent of the silent sufferers of mental illness are not being treated suggests that we, as a profession, must devise innovative ways to reach out to them and let them know what help is available (Regier et al., 1984). It is incumbent upon psychiatrists to address this unmet need; the media represents a readily available and promising avenue of approach.

This case example demonstrates clearly how a call-in show can serve to achieve the ends outlined in Chapter 2. It can play a major role in educating the public about mental illness. It can disseminate information about the cost to society of mental illness. It can advocate for the mentally ill with their families, with legislators, and with the media at large. It can reinforce the availability of mental health services and clarify the psychiatrist's role in the treatment of the mentally ill. And, finally, it can help to improve the image of psychiatry and psychiatrists in general. In this way, a call-in radio show has the potential for encouraging people appropriately to seek help early in the course of a problem, thus helping to improve the overall mental health of the community.

4

RELUCTANCE AND RESISTANCES

To move with confidence into the public media arena, psychiatrists must first understand their own reluctances to take on this responsibility. As is true of any resistance to change, hesitations in this matter pertain to ideas and beliefs that once may have been valid or useful, but which now encase irrational fears or anachronistic concepts. The following discussion is intended as an exploration rather than as a complete catalog of such obstacles.

Professional Self-Image

Each physician has a professional self-image developed over a lifetime. It may have begun with a family doctor offering personal care during a childhood illness. Later, that same dyadic configuration was the primary—or only—image taught in medical school and postgraduate residency. Psychiatrists spend many hours learning the skills necessary to attend to the individual needs of patients. Long-standing practice and the satisfactions derived from this experience reinforce the image. The professional self-image of individual psychiatrists influences the nature of activities in which each elects to participate. Many physicians, particularly psychiatrists, envisage themselves as part of an intimate physician-patient dyad, which image does not accommodate to less personal professional activities. That professional image may be stretched to allow lectures before the local PTA or school assembly, but not stretched enough to permit participation with an unseen and unknown audience.

In addition, the professional image of those who work or were trained in a traditional psychoanalytic mode is one of anonymity. Public exposure of the psychiatrist's personal views or opinions was thought to compromise his/her ability to function with optimal neutrality. This tradition strengthens the resistance of the psychiatrist to being seen or heard or read about in public media.

Although neither tradition nor our professional image should be ignored, we can reexamine them from the perspective of providing public health education and dispelling inaccurate, stereotyped depictions of psychiatry. For some of us, holding to previous professional images and traditions may still be very important. For others, new or changing professional postures may seem in order.

Confusion of Public Education and Soliciting

Another source of resistance to the use of public media has its roots in the confusion of public education with soliciting patients. There has long existed a medical ethic opposing solicitation and personal aggrandizement. Both the technology available for public education and the ethics of professional marketing have undergone considerable change in recent years. In the minds of many psychiatrists, these changes raise concerns of blurring distinctions between public education and the self-serving enhancement of an organization.

In the past, physicians have refrained from advertising or seeking patients lest they be deemed guilty of exploiting the public. Medical professionals have thought of themselves as dedicated humanitarians, and many have looked upon the practices of business with disdain. Without arguing the merits of this position, we can be aware that today medicine is becoming increasingly industrialized. Simultaneously, there is increasing control by governmental regulation in the public sector and by the demands of corporate business needs in the private sector. Thus, medical professionals can no longer remain completely detached from the marketing world.

Although advertising has received organized medicine's endorsement and marketing has become an essential ingredient of the practice of medicine, the changes in laws that have eliminated prohibitions against physicians' advertising have not changed the attitudes of many physicians on this issue. For many, marketing is a source of conflict. At the same time, we know that medicine has always upheld the promotion of medical services in a generic sense, by such statements as: "Check with your own physician." The prohibitions of organized medicine have been against the soliciting of patient clientele by individuals, not against the promotion of adequate medical care through public education or the clear definition of available services.

Public education can inform the citizenry of available medical services so that they can better judge the extent and nature of their need for them. In practice, this type of education does not differ conceptually from the principles of "public health" or "preventive medicine" we have supported for years. The difference is only in the technology of the various public media and the way the present-day audience relates to it. Educational information offered in a pamphlet left in the doctor's waiting room may have been effective in more simple times and places, but today the same material may not reach the intended audience unless it is presented through newsprint, radio, or TV. A generation that has grown up with twice daily newspapers, illustrated weeklies, and ubiquitous television sets may have limited interest in learning from material that is explicitly "education."

If we, in our profession, are not to lose our image as dedicated humanitarians, we must take the responsibility of addressing educational health needs of a public that is increasingly sophisticated. Today this requires modern techniques and involvement with all public media.

Fear of Appearances

Among a number of realistic fears that may cause resistance to participation in public education are misgivings about how we psychiatrists appear to others. These fears of appearance may take several forms. Frequently, the fear is of appearing foolish. The psychiatrist often assumes—or is placed in—a position of authority.

Wearing this cloak can become a comfortable habit, but it can also lead to avoiding circumstances where that authority might appear threatened or insubstantial.

In the same vein, resistance may arise from fear of appearing ignorant. Many well-read and informed persons use medical terms fluently, but may have little knowledge of their meaning. The psychiatrist may overestimate the extent to which use of terms represents knowledge rather than a quest for knowledge. Members of the press who take understandable pride in their ability to pose questions in medical terms can be intimidating to a psychiatrist little experienced in public media interviews. If psychiatrists fall into the trap of parrying with the press rather than offering information, an opportunity to serve the health needs of the public is missed—and their fear of appearing inept is actualized. This kind of experience can often cause resistance when the psychiatrist is approached again. Another source of resistance comes from the fear that one's colleagues will see one's media involvement as arrogant or vain.

Finally, a related fear results from ignorance of the technical aspects of modern media and the erroneous belief that participating in public educational media events requires an understanding of the technical aspects of media. Many psychiatrists feel that lacking such knowledge will create unpleasant situations. This fear and the subsequent resistance to working with the media are augmented by a common mistaken impression that "all reporters are out to make fools of those whom they interview." Such fears are overcome by the development of skills in working with the media. Suggestions for acquiring appropriate techniques will be discussed in Chapters 5 and 6.

Ethical Concerns

Among the diverse reasons our profession has resisted using the media to promote public education or to define the profession and its capabilities are a group of ethical concerns. Any group that holds itself to be a profession must develop a code of ethics which must be commonly understood within a tolerable latitude of disagreement. Members of the profession must take such standards upon themselves by free choice. Resistance occurs because the psychiatrists' use of the media raises ethical intraprofessional questions that elude easy and commonly held answers. Ethical questions, for example, may surround issues of confidentiality, or whether interview answers that are intended to inform on a radio show constitute a psychiatrist-patient relationship. Avoiding the media altogether may seem easier and less dangerous than trying to tackle associated ethical questions. Avoidance may seem the best solution if possible ethical violations appear to threaten the integrity of those who use the media. Understanding these ethical questions enables psychiatrists to make informed choices.

Confidentiality

Issues of confidentiality may become problematic, even threatening, in approaching public education through the media. The ethical requirement of holding in confidence what we hear from our patients in the course of our work with them has always been central to the medical profession. On this there is general agreement. Clearly ethical considerations do not allow us to illustrate a point by recognizably describing a patient who is or was in treatment with us. Our intraprofessional presentation of scientific case reports requires great care to prevent identification of a particular person. But this need not prevent our translating our experientially gained knowledge in a general, nonidentifying manner for the educational benefit of the public.

The issue can come into sharper focus on radio or TV talk shows when someone calls the psychiatrist on the air to discuss a problem or symptom. As always, the privilege of confidentiality belongs to the patient rather than the physician. By calling in on a public medium, that caller makes a decision about the confidential nature (or lack of it) of the interaction. The psychiatrist may choose to avoid material that might be embarrassing or harmful to the caller and may defer to a later, more private interaction by telephone or letter. That option, however, is an additional sensitivity which can be brought to the interchange by the psychiatrist. It does not create a situation demanding confidentiality. The caller does not become a "patient" either ethically or legally simply by virtue of calling the program. The essential difference lies in the fact that although the psychiatrist may conduct a professional interaction with a listener/caller, the psychiatrist-patient configuration strictly exists only when a therapeutic contract is implicit.

Information/Education vs. Therapeutic Advice

Another common issue of professional ethics concerns the differences between information/education and therapeutic advice. There are ethical differences between information or education on one hand and therapeutic advice on the other. Maintaining this distinction, of course, is not simple. Any comments by a psychiatrist about issues of health or disease could be construed to be therapeutic advice, and often the caller is requesting specific advice. The ethical distinction appears to lie in a recognition of the context in which advice is being sought. Direct advice given to a caller with the specific intent of treating the symptom or ailment under discussion would be very different from an exploration of the problem in order to enlighten a wide listening audience on subjects raised by a caller. In either case, the caller benefits from the discussion. But in the latter context, ethics of treatment do not apply. Rather than representing a form of treatment, the talk show format aims at educating the audience. Medical ethics require responsible attention to professional conduct, but they need not deter us from teaching.

Public Interest or Self-Interest

In some arguments, the careful separation of public interest from self-interest is basic to any medical ethical considerations. This dichotomy may be particularly necessary in using the media, necessary not only to protect the public, but also to protect the psychiatrist involved. An example of a dilemma that may arise relates to the question of whether psychiatrists should treat people who want to come to them as patients after having seen or heard them in the media. Although this is uncommon, the would-be patient is often insistent upon being seen by that particular doctor and can be very persuasive. Often, having very positive feelings, the person is seeking treatment with magical expectations of the psychiatrist's capabilities. The chances of either psychiatrist or patient coming out of that situation satisfactorily are probably very slight without the intervening ethical principles that prohibit raising unrealistic treatment expectations. Ethical guidelines, thus, do not prohibit physicians from public media visibility; they make it effectively and professionally possible without harming the psychiatrist or exploiting the public.

Very closely related to the concern about self-interest is the resistance that may arise out of the fear that the professional will be seen by colleagues as neither professional nor educator, but only as a self-serving entertainer. Indeed, that line is easy to cross at times because good education can be entertaining and good educators can develop a degree of fame, or notoriety, in their own right. Some of the problems might be circumvented by insisting that those who speak for the profession be limited to representatives who are elected by their peers or to colleagues who are involved in public service, administration, or education. These guidelines may be helpful, but are not entirely free of controversy either. In the end, this resistance probably will be overcome only by careful adherence to professional standards by media educators and by careful tolerance of individual differences by professional colleagues.

In summary, a variety of concerns inhibit individual psychiatrists from interacting with the media. One's professional self-image, distaste for soliciting, fears of appearing foolish or ignorant, uncertainty over ethical ramifications, and the fear of colleagues' criticism can effect formidable resistances to meeting the media. However, when closely examined, many of the fears are exposed as irrelevant to the task, ungrounded, or surmountable through minimal coaching. If we overcome unnecessary resistances, we are free to use the public media for the worthy purpose of public education, which will include both education about matters of mental health/illness needs and a more concise definition of the psychiatric services available to meet those needs.

5

MEETING THE MEDIA

Psychiatrists commonly feel anxious and afraid of their initial contacts with the media. The experience can be compared with acting as an expert witness in court. The physician is away from his or her usual environment, is attempting to convey complex concepts to a lay audience, and the interviewer is perceived, sometimes correctly, as the hostile adversary. The feeling that you are representing not only yourself, but also the practice of psychiatry and medicine, adds to your sense of responsibility. In discussions with any media person, be certain to clarify whether you are voicing your own opinions or acting as a spokesperson for an institution or organization. Your role is critical to the public education process. As an expert in the field of psychiatry, you have the credibility to present ideas and information about this important aspect of health care. It is essential in talking to media representatives to let them know you are a psychiatrist *and* a physician. If quoted, be sure to have "M.D." listed after your name. Reporters and interviewers can be your conduits, summarizing the story you tell or helping you to present your information to the public.

Establishing rapport with the media person is challenging. Probably you have never met the person before and will not have an ongoing relationship with that person. The media person may have a personal interest in and may have done extensive research on a given subject and may pose very sophisticated questions. Or, the reporter may be ignorant regarding the subject matter or have inaccurate information. You, as the psychiatrist, must determine the level of knowledge of the reporter and address your comments to parallel the reporter's understanding of the topic. You should offer to provide written background to the reporter or refer the media person to other sources of information.

Try to familiarize yourself with your potential audience and the audience of the reporter. All media prosper on their ability to hold regular audiences. The size of the audience determines, in part, the impact of an article or program. Interest of the audience, as perceived by the editor or program producer, determines how much coverage, space and time is given. To a large degree, the audience's deemed philosophy determines how a subject is handled. An urban daytime television interview will reach a different population than an article in a magaizne.

Preparing for an Interview

In addition to knowing your audience, if possible, learn something of the background of the interviewer or reporter. Reporters have idiosyncratic knowledge, opinions and attitudes about subjects and issues which are likely to influence how they may treat a subject in printed article or broadcast interview. They definitely determine the types of questions, the way they are asked, and the tone in which they are asked. Some reporters and interviewers aggressively pursue their subjects; many more are low-key and simply want to explore a topic. To respond effectively, you must be thoroughly prepared before the interview.

To learn the editorial position of a publication or program, and the way that reporters have treated recent issues, scan back copies of the publications or monitor several broadcasts of the program. Newspapers maintain "morgues" or files of past articles. When watching or listening to a television or radio show before your appearance, pay special attention to the host's approach to the guest, the tone, the style of questioning, and the attitudes toward issues. If the format is a debate or panel discussion, pay particular attention to the way that the moderator handles varying points of view or moves the conversation from one panelist to another.

After you have researched your audience and evaluated the possible approach the host or reporter will take, prepare yourself to answer questions as directly and concisely as possible. For quick reference, Appendix 2 offers "Sample Brief Answers to Commonly Asked Questions" and Appendix 3 consists of "Fact Sheets" on many mental health topics. Most hospitals and universities have public relations staff who can help you in dealing with the media. You can improve your media style through "mock interviews" recorded on audio- or videotape, followed by critical review of the performance by the public relations staff.

The Brief Statement

You should have one or two specific communication objectives for each interview, both broadcast and print. By determining the objective in advance and keeping it in mind during the interview, you will be less likely to wander off the track and more likely to achieve your communications goal. Having a specific agenda in mind allows you to emphasize your statement. Emphasizing a limited number of key points, will enable your audience to remember them if nothing else is remembered from your interview. During the interview, always keep your one or two points in mind and seek opportunities to return to them whenever possible.

It is important to help reporters with the accuracy of the material and to avoid being misquoted. One way this can be accomplished is providing the reporter with a written statement, news release, or background article before the interview and giving him or her a chance to read it before you begin. Not being hasty, clearly defining your terms and restating the statement to be sure the reporter understands, is helpful in maintaining accuracy. If you sense that the reporter is still missing the point, say, "I should emphasize that the main point is . . . " You can ask the reporter to restate from his notes key points or technical information to make certain that you both agree on his understanding of the material you have covered. If you believe the reporter is trying to put words into your mouth, say, "I am not saying that; what I am saying is . . . " Then continue by restating the points that you want to make. Above all, stick to your topic.

You may be called on to comment on many kinds of topics, whether they seem related to psychiatry or not. Psychiatrists have been asked to explain reactions to catastrophes, the stock market and rock groups, and render opinions on such matters as birth control, abortion or capital punishment. Sometimes even more controversial topics come up. The press these days is interested in the insanity defense and its use and abuse, the lack or need of mental hospital care, and the efficacy of psychiatry. No question from the media should be ignored. The best way of dealing with nonpsychiatric topics is to provide a brief and very general response and then attempt to lead the interviewer to a more appropriate area of discussion. It is unethical to offer an opinion or diagnosis of a public figure or an individual in the news unless you have conducted an examination and have been granted proper authorization for such a statement. You must protect the confidentiality of your patients. You may refer to *Guidelines for Psychiatrists Working with the Communications Media* (see Appendix 1).

The 20-Second Answer

Be factual, knowledgeable, and brief. Some questions do not have simple answers; some comments do not require a response. "I don't know" is preferable to inaccurate speculation. To say "No comment" in response to a question may be seen as hostile. A better strategy is to explain why it would not be positive to respond. Do not be afraid to state that you do not have sufficient expertise in a given area, and if possible, to refer to someone who does. When asked to comment on a specific individual or incident, explain that you do not have the information to make a judgment, and/or that to comment would breach confidentiality. Use common lay terms rather than complicated scientific jargon. Sometimes the use of similes will help convey ideas, but they must be used carefully due to the potential for misinterpretation. An example of a good simile is: "Bipolar disorder is like an emotional roller coaster with extreme highs and lows." If asked a provocative or complex question, it is appropriate to use such statements or qualifiers as: "There is no clear-cut answer to your question; however, some clinicians feel . . . " or "Controversy still exists regarding that issue, but in general the evidence shows . . . " or "You have asked a complex question, let me address it in phases. . . . " As a policy, you should not believe media people who tell you that they will not quote you on a question or ask you to speak off the record. Psychiatrists' off-the-record responses frequently seem to end up public knowledge. Reporters can misunderstand, change your emphasis, or misinterpret your statements. They rarely do so intentionally. It happens because they are not familiar with your subject or because you have not taken adequate steps to help them understand the material. Although anything you say may appear in print or on the air, most media experiences will be with journalists who are intelligent, ethical and honest.

General Tips for a Successful Interview

Take time to prepare for the interview, and consider the questions to be asked. Brush up on facts and figures. Keep the reporter's deadline in mind and return the reporter's phone calls promptly. Determine your subject, then help tie together the interview by working your theme into your answers to the questions. Rather than providing a one-word response to questions, amplify your answers to assist the reporter in getting the story. Show consideration for the reporter and his or her objectives. Take the time to explain the technicalities or even the basics of your subject, taking into account the public's viewpoint. Identify anything you say as fact or speculation, being careful to separate the two. Avoid picking up negative phrasing from the reporter. If the reporter asks, "Why haven't you found a cure for . . . ?" answer, "We now have effective treatments for . . . " It is important to correct misinformation and always to tell the truth. Speak clearly and simply and avoid excessive or complicated medical terminology. The more easily the reporter is able to grasp your meaning, the greater the chance you will not be misunderstood or misquoted. Avoid discussing hypothetical situations, and avoid commenting, except as a concerned ordinary citizen, on subjects outside your area of professional expertise. Remember, good reporters, especially those who write about medicine, are just as interested in telling the story accurately as you are and want to maintain a good working relationship with their sources.

Dealing with the Hostile Interviewer

The interviewer can express hostility through style or content. The rapid-fire interviewer throws multiple questions at you from the outset and throughout the interaction. This person can be handled in a number of ways:

1. Mention that he or she has asked a number of questions and ask the host to restate one question.
2. Note that the interviewer has asked several questions and request that he or she choose which one you should answer first.
3. Pick the question you like and give a complete answer.

The interviewer who constantly interrupts can derail you from conveying your primary message. Techniques for handling such a person include:

1. Ignore the interruption, complete your answer, then ask the interviewer to repeat the question.
2. Stop what you were saying, allow the interviewer to finish the question, then explain that you will answer the new question next.
3. Consider that you may be rambling and the interviewer may be trying to help direct you back to the subject at hand.

The interviewer may present questions with distorted and inflammatory content, for example, "Why do you psychiatrists control people's minds with tranquilizers?" These questions must be dealt with in a level-headed, objective manner. Your response might be, "There are specific medications for specific disorders that help some people obtain relief from the suffering of mental illness. A tranquilizer is one of these which is used to help relieve emotional symptoms." Try not to lose your temper when dealing with the hostile interviewer. Never walk out of an interview. If you can deal with this type of interviewer so that you come across as a sincere, knowledgeable, ethical psychiatrist, your resultant self-esteem will enable you to communicate clearly with the media audience.

6

DEALING WITH THE MEDIA

Newspapers

Newspapers, the oldest form of mass media in this country, are the medium most likely to cover events in the field of psychiatry. Their audience tends to be broad based and undefined. There is selective readership, that is, each person reads only that what interests him or her. Nonetheless, editors try to engage and sustain the interest of all readers with each story. To the extent they succeed, they reach an audience most diverse.

Although they have entertainment features—comics, puzzles, editorials, fashion tips, columns—newspapers focus on news. Generally, the news must be timely (its value is diminished if delayed) and of significance to its reader. Events are deemed more significant if they occur locally or in some way affect the reader directly. If they involve a prominent personality, conflict, a natural disaster or, something of "human interest," they are newsworthy. Psychiatry often makes the news when a sensational crime or bizarre behavior causes news reporters to wonder about the perpetrator's mental health. Specialized science writers are more likely to write about an advance in psychiatry or a new public policy affecting the mentally ill.

There is limited space in a newspaper. The number of pages to an issue is determined by the amount of advertising obtained. The editors determine what will go into the paper. The owner/publisher or editor-in-chief sets policy and establishes the tone for the paper as a whole. Ideally, advertisers do not influence the way news is reported. In large city newspapers with a loyal following, the advertisers may need the coverage more than the paper needs their support.

Small local papers may be less independent, since 55 to 70 percent of their income is from advertising.

Depending on the size of the newspaper, editors as well as reporters will be more or less specialized. In a major city newspaper, not only will there be a Health Science editor and several medical reporters, there may be a reporter who covers mental health issues only. Such reporters cover changes in government policy affecting mental health, incidents that occur within the local mental health system, and breakthroughs in the treatment or understanding of mental illness. In addition to daily news articles, they write feature stories or series that may or may not relate to news events. The subjects for most of these stories are decided in the editorial offices, but medical reporters and editors are open to suggestions; for example, a psychiatrist may mention a newsworthy psychiatric event or topic to a reporter with whom he has worked, and the reporter may follow up on the lead.

Reporters who are experienced in the area of mental health will often be on good terms with several psychiatrists. When writing a story, they are likely to contact these psychiatrists first for information. The psychiatrists may then refer them to colleagues more familiar with that subject. Reporters may also call individuals whose names are prominent in the literature for the subject being treated. If public policy is at issue, the appropriate government officials may be contacted.

Newspaper coverage has several strengths. It can provide more details than television or radio and is, therefore, better suited to explain complex issues. Readers can go back if they miss a key point; they can reread an article of interest, or clip it for later reference. Most importantly, newspapers have tremendous credibility. We believe what we read more than what we hear: "It's in black and white."

Newspaper "How To's"

Newspaper interviews can be less stressful than radio or television because the psychiatrist is not directly observed and can clarify and elaborate on certain points. However, newspaper reporters seldom come back or call for clarification; therefore, it is vital to be as clear and succinct as possible when first in contact with them. In talking to a reporter, keep explanations simple and straightforward. The newspaper's task is to present the public with technical or complex information in an easily understandable way.

Reporters are constantly on deadline and may have only a few hours to research, interview, and write a story. Depending upon the publication and the type of article, the deadline may vary from a few hours to a week. Dailies usually have an afternoon deadline. Contact with these reporters is often by phone. They may need information immediately and be unable to wait for a return call. If you are returning a call, have all your information at hand. Try to be as brief as reasonable, and to the point.

Because articles for newspaper feature sections require more research, the deadlines are longer than those for the general news section of daily papers. The story resulting from an interview may not appear for several days or several weeks. Nonetheless, there is still an urgency to the interview. Like their news counterparts, feature writers frequently work on a story under deadline pressure.

Newspaper feature interviews are frequently conducted face-to-face. The feature writer will be looking for as much anecdotal information as possible. A feature story is built around personalities, good quotes, interesting anecdotes, unusual information, and solid facts. Like most reporters, the feature writer is not likely to be an expert on your subject and will look to you for information. If possible, have the reporter call back and read the story to you or send a prepublication draft for you to proofread for accuracy.

If you have an idea for an article, contact either the medical editor or one of the medical reporters by phone. Editors receive copy from many sources outside their staff. If you have written a piece you would like published in a newspaper, it should be neatly typed, with a heading to indicate what it is about, and with your identity clearly stated.

Television

Television transmits sight and sound simultaneously, drawing the audience into the scene. Television dramatizes, arouses interest and creates atmosphere in a way akin to theater. It captures the audience. Viewers rarely engage in other activities while watching.

Although potentially very profitable, television is an expensive medium to operate. It had traditionally been dominated by national networks. Cable television, initially supported solely by subscription, has become increasingly popular and more commercialized. Originally, in order to break into the market, these stations limited their offerings. Some specialize in a defined genre in hopes of serving a given segment of the viewing public; this is called "narrowcasting." There are significant distinctions between commercial television and local subscriber programming. Local programming is likely to be less professional. We will focus on commercial television, since it is still the mainstay of American broadcasting.

Except for public broadcasting stations, TV networks depend entirely on advertising for their income. Their sponsors may not care about the content of a program if it draws large audiences. The name of the game is ratings. To win, producers learn all they can about their potential audience. From companies like Nielsen, they learn more than the relative popularity of programs. Analyses of who watches what and when, include the age, sex and interests of viewers. With this in mind, producers program material they believe will maintain and enlarge their public. Since many homes have a limited number of television sets, family members often compromise on what to watch. Educational or specialty programming frequently loses out to pure "entertainment" with broad-based appeal—both in the home and in the producer's office.

Television broadcasts require triple the amount of time radio broadcasts take to plan and execute. As a result of the expense, local producers can rarely afford to take risks. Most stations are network affiliates. They fill much of their air time with syndicated programming designed to satisfy varying audiences nationwide.

While the networks have more financial leeway to experiment, they tend to be cautious. PBS has been innovative in the content and format of its programming. Presumably, this is because its stations are nonprofit, their funding source is somewhat diversified, and their income is not dependent solely on the numbers of viewers they attract. Corporations, organizations and individuals are willing to support the production of valuable educational and/or artistic programs, even if they may not attract as wide an audience as conventional broadcasts.

Locally produced news programs are the most likely to consult a psychiatrist. Television news is slower paced than radio because both visual and auditory stimuli need to register. There may be time for slightly more coverage than in radio. Nevertheless, only 40 to 90 seconds are generally allotted for a news story and as little as 15 to 20 seconds for an interview.

Psychiatrists have also been guests on television talk shows. The producers of these shows receive innumerable suggestions for each segment of their broadcasts. Such a show is likely to have an associate producer who handles health-related material. The associate producer is responsible for judging what within the health field is of interest to the audience, and determines what will be aired, subject to the producer's approval.

If one is to appear on the air, it is helpful to be familiar with television studios. They tend to be small and crowded. The lights are bright and hot. Studios contain two or three cameras, presentation aids, and studio monitors for the production crew. Televised guests do not look at the monitors except while presenting films or slides.

Four to six production staff may be in the studio. The guest is only concerned with the floor manager. It is the floor manager who communicates the director's instructions. (The director is in the control room.) The type of microphone used depends on the nature of the program. Talk show guests frequently wear microphones. Alternatively, a "table mike" may be present.

Those who prepare television presentations think visually. As a rule of thumb, audiences are interested in seeing people and action. However, if poorly planned, the visual component will be distracting. Television viewers are sophisticated, accustomed to seeing the best. They are critical of anything less than professional.

Television is a difficult medium with which to work. Not only the subject matter, but the way it is presented, one's speaking voice and one's appearance are all significant. Commercial television is also very competitive—with good reason. It is potentially the most powerful of the media. Millions are reached instantaneously and are profoundly influenced: "Seeing is believing."

Television "How-To's"

Television provides an opportunity to be seen and heard directly by the audience. It is possible to present facts and establish credibility with poise, gestures, intonation, delivery, speed and appearance. If not taken into consideration and utilized properly, these visual and audio effects can weaken the impact of your interview. It should be emphasized that your appearance will probably determine your credibility and how well the information you offer will be retained.

Many TV stations have the potential to put an "overlay" on the film with the physician's name and title. This information can be given to the interviewer on a 3″ × 5″ card or business card to ensure correct spelling and accuracy. Example: John Doe, M.D., Psychiatrist; or John Doe, M.D.

Television is a seeing medium so consider what is visual about your subject and emphasize it. The more action there is—such as people conducting research or equipment in use—the better for background shots. Any visual aids to be used must be discussed in advance with the show's producer.

Brevity is the key to TV interviews. Although you may be interviewed for 20 minutes, only 30 seconds may end up on the air. If possible, try to open the interview with a succinct summary that tells your story best. Opening statements alert the viewers to what is coming since they cannot go back to what was missed. Thereafter, speak in short sentences. That makes the editing process easier for the reporters. Use interesting, simple language. The viewer will be seeing and hearing you only once. Share your enthusiasm with the reporter and ultimately the viewer.

If you are to be interviewed on the air, learn ahead of time where you fit in the program, who is the audience, and what type of questions your host will ask. Frequently a staff person will contact you in advance to review this material. Television interviews are usually more rushed and involve greater time pressure than those with the printed media. It helps to have a "dry run" or a chance to talk with the interviewers for a few minutes before the show begins. This allows the psychiatrist to establish rapport, decrease anxiety, and anticipate the type of interview that will be conducted. You will not be allowed to use notes during the interview. Unless otherwise instructed, while on camera, the psychiatrist should look at the interviewer and follow the interviewer's lead.

Relaxation is the key to success. You should avoid becoming defensive or antagonistic. Anticipation and preparation can be very useful in knowing the points that you want to get across or in expecting key questions that you might be asked. Be prepared to use those questions as launching pads for your communication objectives. Anticipate potentially negative questions and prepare responses that focus on positive points. Being sincere and telling the truth is the best approach. Try, if rational, to end each answer on a positive note.

If you are being interviewed on a news show, your comments are going to be limited so it is essential to get your ideas across in approximately 20 to 30 seconds. You will have to use a minimum of well-chosen words. If you are lucky, you may get one minute. You should try to answer questions in one sentence. Each reply should be a self-contained message. In that way, in case the interview is being taped, the context of your message will not be lost when the tape is edited. How long you will have to answer your questions will depend on the type of show, where the interview is taking place, whether it is being taped, taped live, or broadcast live. The taped interview may last as long as 10 to 15 minutes, but most of what you say will remain on the cutting room floor. Your actual appearance will probably be only a minute or two. When you are taped live, a tape is being made for editing while you are being interviewed live. Portions of this interview may be rebroadcast at a later date or time. A live interview on the news broadcast is the shortest. The audience sees and hears you exactly as you are talking.

If you would like to be a guest on a television talk show, contact the associate producer who handles health and science. He or she will determine whether the presentation you propose is suitable for television and whether it is of interest to the viewers.

The following are suggestions that will help you to come across in the best possible way during a television appearance:

1. Dress conservatively. Avoid shiny materials, vivid and intricate patterns, bold stripes, and the color white. Women should avoid wearing shiny makeup. Tinted lenses in glasses should be avoided if possible.
2. Arrive at the studio at least 15 minutes before showtime unless otherwise notified.
3. Don't worry if someone wants to apply a little powder to your face or adjust an article of your clothing. That person is only interested in making you look better.
4. Sit upright in the chair with your legs together or crossed toward the interviewer so that the camera doesn't show the bottom of your shoes. Men should wear over-the-calf socks.
5. Ignore the audience and concentrate on the interviewer. This will be a more comfortable way of relating for you; psychiatrists are usually more at ease with a one-to-one dialogue.
6. Never look at the camera unless you are given specific instructions to do so. Make eye contact with the interviewer. Avoid watching yourself on the monitor.
7. Feel free to gesture, but keep your pertinent movements fairly close to your body. Avoid nervous gestures like wringing your hands, gripping your chair, or swinging your leg.
8. When the interview is over, stay seated until the interviewer

stands. The show isn't over until the camera stops rolling. The microphone is always on.

9. Try to relax and enjoy the interview. This is the most difficult advice to follow, especially if it is your first time on camera. But keep in mind that you have something newsworthy and interesting and, you intend, educational, to share with the viewer. If you firmly believe in what you are saying, the audience will respect your opinion. It is important to come across as believable.

Radio

The very phrase "psychiatrists and the media" conjures up the image of a radio talk show host, answering calls about sexual impotence or unruly adolescents. In fact, only an estimated two dozen professionals nationwide have successful mental health shows on the air. Although such programming is in vogue, the opportunities are extremely limited. In general, radio is a unique medium with requirements psychiatrists only sometimes satisfy.

Radio electronically transmits sound over a distance to millions of receivers. Yet, it is a peculiarly personal medium, duplicating a one-to-one situation between speaker and listener. Broadcasts are heard 24 hours a day in every conceivable location, usually while the listener engages in some other activity. Reliance must be upon auditory stimuli alone to hold the listener's interest. The pace is rapid. Anything missed is irretrievably lost. Thus, it may not be well suited to detailed explanations. Radio does stimulate, motivate and titillate. It can educate, but its impact may be fleeting and/or trivial.

In the United States, radio stations are primarily dependent on advertisers for their subsidization. Attracting and keeping sponsors is a never-ending struggle. Of course, the way to succeed is by attracting and keeping large audiences. The competition is intense, with most cities having several AM and FM stations. Almost all programming today is done locally. In order to survive, many stations have evolved specialized roles, servicing a specific subpopulation that will be loyal. For instance, a station may focus on one type of music, or may be "all talk." Large established stations are more likely to provide a traditional mix of news, music, talk and so forth. Whichever niche a radio station fills, its principal objective is to attract many listeners.

Radio personalities tend to be "showmen." More than articulate, they are theatrical, perhaps glib. Usually they exude warmth or, at least, arouse emotion in their listeners. Their choice of subject matter is based on what is marketable.

Some psychiatrists have a talent for broadcasting. They are the ones who can host talk shows. Facile talkers with pleasing speaking voices, they can capture the public's interest by talking about issues with general appeal. Relationships, marriage, sex, gambling, alcoholism, are issues which touch large segments of the population, and, therefore, hold their interest. They are also socially acceptable problems. A discussion of schizophrenia or clinical depression may turn some listeners away. Unfortunately, some radio programs prefer to serve only light, easily digestible fare.

To succeed with a program that is aired regularly, there has to be an adequate reservoir of new information. Due to its rapid pace and superficial coverage, radio consumes information at a tremendous rate. The "media shrink" taps his or her audience to fill this demand. Callers from the audience keep talk shows fresh and interesting. Newscasts or other programs often add interest and variety by interviewing guests on the air. The guests are often authorities chosen for their special knowledge and need not be "personalities."

Many of today's syndicated talk show hosts started by attracting a large following while with a local station. However, there are many, many more interested professionals than there are opportunities for air time. On the other hand, as was mentioned, radio stations are hungry for material to air on existing programs. A program or news director is likely to welcome well thought-out suggestions for a guest appearance or feature story.

Radio has several strengths as a medium. It reaches tremendous numbers of people with the immediacy of personal contact. It provides up-to-the-minute coverage. For the field of psychiatry, radio's informality provides a special advantage. The familiarity and comfort listeners feel with their station will be extended to the radio psychiatrist. This, in turn, can diminish fear and distrust felt toward the mental health profession in general.

Radio "How To's"

Radio interviews may be 15 minutes or longer. However, radio news interviews often last between two and three minutes. Therefore, providing simple straightforward information is even more important than it is for newspaper interviews. Interviewer and guest should review ahead of time how the guest fits into the program, what the interviewer wants to bring into focus, how the interview will begin, and how the guest will know when it is ending. Some radio programs are taped ahead of time. If one has good rapport with the host, the host will often allow sections of the interview to be retaped if the original is somehow inadequate.

The radio news reporter's tool is the tape recorder, a device that can record almost as well over the telephone as in person. Since radio reporters often need their stories immediately, many ask to conduct their interviews by phone rather than in person.

Whether a radio interview is conducted in person or over the phone, it is helpful to remember that delivery is extremely important. You must rely totally on your tone of voice to emhasize key points in answering questions since radio depends only on sound to create mental images for its listeners.

If one is invited to speak on the air, it is important to be reliable and punctual. Radio shows go on exactly as scheduled, whether or not the guest has arrived. There is no way to add or make up time. Also, remember that radio is a personal medium. While on the air, one should picture the audience as one or two friendly listeners.

Occasionally, a psychiatrist has the skills and interest to host his or her own show. If you want your own radio show, you must convince a local station that you can devleop and maintain an audience. You should mail a coherent presentation of your suggested format to every radio station in town. The program directors should be called as well. If interested, a director will judge after meeting you whether he feels you have the voice and charisma to succeed.

On a radio call-in show, delivery is probably the key issue. It is important to show concern for the caller and his/her problems. Advice should not be provided to a member of the studio or listening audience that could be considered as therapy or treatment. A diagnosis should not be stated or the problem described in any conclusive way. The host should ask the caller questions that would help obtain additional information which then leads to comments about broad topics such as depression or substance abuse. It is appropriate to suggest referrals such as an initial evaluation by a primary care physician or a psychiatrist.

Most call-in shows can be managed very well, but on rare occasions the psychiatrist must deal with difficult and provocative callers. A few tips will make this kind of experience smoother:

1. Do not be uneasy at the prospect of handling "crank" or "crackpot" calls. There is usually a time lapse between the time the caller addresses you and the time the comment is heard by the listening audience. This allows the engineer to "edit" what is broadcast and any inappropriate or obscene commentary is removed.
2. Always be on your toes. If is often difficult to determine whether a caller has finished a question or commentary or is simply pausing and intends to continue. You must not allow too much time to lapse before answering, but neither should you be hasty and possibly interrupt a complete question or thought.
3. Do not let the caller "bully" you. You should not allow yourself to be baited into inadvertently criticizing a person or concept you choose not to criticize. Given the anonymity in which callers can express themselves on radio call-in shows, listeners can become extremely aggressive.
4. Some callers delight in upsetting the guest on call-in shows. Always keep your emotions in check. An alert moderator will

not allow the situation to get out of hand. If you feel your composure beginning to slip, suggest to the moderator moving on to the next call.

Magazines

The first American magazine was published by Benjamin Franklin in 1741. However, the wild success of commercial magazines is a phenomenon of the last century. More than 300 new magazines are introduced each year. Most magazines are more or less specialized, catering to a particular interest or a specific segment of the population. Fashion, sports, news, science and gossip are some of the themes around which a periodical may be organized. Members of a given age group, sex, and/or lifestyle are targeted.

Accordingly, as magazines target a specific audience, the extent of their impact is limited. By the same token, their articles can be focused and, therefore, succeed in holding their readers' interest. The psychiatrist frequently may seek to communicate with one segment of the population, for example, to enlighten teenaged women about eating disorders or parents of young children about enuresis. One addresses the appropriate audience by publishing in the right magazine. Impact is enhanced by not trying to satisfy a diverse population.

Magazine staffs vary widely in size. The publisher is the ultimate boss. The editor, the circulation manager, the advertising manager, the overseer of the printing plant, and the head of promotions and public relations all answer to the publisher. The editor, in turn, oversees the editorial staff and acts as liaison with the aforementioned parties. The executive or managing editor is responsible for screening all the work submitted. There may be a number of associate editors under the executive editor. The art director is in charge of the pictorial components. In addition, there may be staff writers or contributing editors, who often write a portion of a magazine's copy.

Magazines make 45 to 60 percent of their income from advertising; the rest comes from subscriptions and newsstand sales. Circulation is the decisive factor. It follows that editors are judged by their ability to assess and satisfy the interests of their audience. That is the ultimate criterion for determining what articles to print. More and more, publishers are investing in research to aid editors in evaluating the tastes of audiences.

The key element of a publishable magazine article is the idea being communicated. It must be fresh, original, and preferably, upbeat. If an exciting idea that a psychiatrist submits results in being a successful published article, publishers may subsequently court the psychiatrist. Several bestselling authors have first attracted recognition by writing magazine articles.

Commercial magazines have many strengths as a communications medium. They have the credibility of print with the added emotional zing of photography. In writing for a magazine, one has the time and space for in-depth coverage. Analyses of complex subject matter may be undertaken when of interest to a selected audience able and willing to spend time studying the article and/or referring back to it. Of course, the writing must capture and hold the readers' attention. For a psychiatrist who can transmit exciting thoughts and write well, or who collaborates with an experienced writer, magazines may be the best medium for reaching members of the lay public.

Magazine "How To's"

If you possess literary talent, you may want to attempt magazine writing, which is a special skill. Professional organizations such as NIH and the APA have sponsored workshops on writing techniques. Numerous how-to books for prospective journalists are in libraries. The monthly periodical, *Writers' Digest,* should also be consulted.

Writers' Yearbook, published annually, lists publications and evaluates their major markets. *Writer's Market,* in addition, lists the staff of publications, so you can look up whom to contact with the idea for a story. Of course, you should never write to a magazine editor until familiar with the periodical. In order to understand the type of material the magazine publishes, read at least three of its issues.

Once you have decided which magazine should publish your article, submit a query letter to the Articles Editor or his or her equivalent. *Writers' Market* lists who acts as gatekeeper for each periodical, along with his or her title. Your query letter tells what your proposed article will be about, presents your credentials, and, most importantly, is designed to capture the editor's interest. Hitting hard and coming right to the point sells a writer's product. Query letters are short, preferably not more than a page. Specifics about the story, facts and figures, along with provocative statements should be included. However, do not tell the entire story. The editor, it may be hoped, will want to read the article. At the end of the letter, give your credentials, particularly your writing credits. It is advisable to read an article or textbook chapter on writing query letters before attempting your first few.

Some say that there are situations in which query letters are not appropriate. They suggest that when a writer has no journalistic credentials, is absolutely unable to write a good query letter, or is submitting a very short piece, the work itself should be mailed to the articles editor. This is a matter of judgment. Never call an editor unless he or she is a personal friend. Editors will only be irritated by such interruptions in their hectic schedules. If you plan to work with a collaborator, inform the editor in advance and give the collaborator's credentials in your query letter. Do not expect a magazine to assign a writer to your proposed story; magazines do not usually have sufficient staff.

Even psychiatrists with little interest in journalism may be interviewed for a magazine. Magazine interviews are more likely to be face-to-face than over the telephone. Magazines are interested in covering all facets of a topic. You, as an expert on the subject, are expected to provide information. Magazine interviews are generally an hour or more in length and thorough in nature. The publication's editor is likely to ask for a comprehensive article on a given subject.

Magazines have long lead times and reporters work many months, even a year, in advance of publication. The interview given today may not be published for several months. However, it will result in a story that may reach an audience of millions. You may request and be sent a publication copy of the article for review and for your records.

Syndicated Features

Another attractive option for the psychiatrist who wishes to publish is writing for a newspaper syndicate. You can write and submit an article on whatever subject you think would be of interest. If the editors can sell the article to newspapers (or magazines), they will divide the profits evenly with you. You can also arrange with a syndicate to write a regular column. Publishing through a syndicate allows you to reach a geographically dispersed audience, and may be less competitive than trying to publish in a commercial magazine. A listing of news services and feature syndicates, with names, addresses and phone numbers of whom to contact can be found in the annual *Literary Market Place.* Most general reference libraries will have a copy.

Mass media, whether print or broadcast, offer psychiatrists the opportunity to educate large segments of the lay public. Armed with a rudimentary understanding of the media and a few tips on how to interact with reporters, editors and talk show hosts, the psychiatrist can effectively communicate expertise to a wide audience.

CONCLUSION

Effective collaboration and use of the media require that psychiatrists develop a working knowledge of the mass communications field. Psychiatrists should appreciate the requirements of the media for information and respond in terms that are accurate and understandable.

There are many potential benefits to developing a strategy of public education through more effective use of the media. Increased visibility of and familiarity with modern psychiatry through positive media exposure will help dispel negative stereotypes. Emphasis on the unique role of the psychiatrist as physician and mental health professional will improve the appropriate use of services. Public knowledge about mental illness will increase recognition of problems and reduce the stigma and denial that interferes with seeking treatment. As informed consumers, the public will be better able to seek help when needed and evaluate the quality of services provided.

An informed public can apply pressure on third party payers to reverse the current trend toward reduced mental health benefits. They can become able and inclined to participate in policy decisions regarding the provision of mental health services. Recent research documents the high prevalence of mental illness, underutilization of available services, and, at the same time, an urgent need for psychiatric and supportive care services at present and in the future. The support of the public will be essential if we are to realize more effective systems of mental health care.

This handbook addresses how psychiatrists can most effectively be involved in public education and thus reduce ignorance and negative attitudes concerning mental illness. The various forms of the mass media, the part they play in molding public policy, and some of psychiatry's failures to take full advantage of the opportunities media offer have been discussed. The handbook represents a basic guide to effective interactions with the media. The goals of contemporary clinical psychiatry and the future of our profession demand that psychiatrists respond to their public responsibilities. Our intent is not to encourage or expect every psychiatrist to seek out media contact or exposure. Psychiatrists with experience, interest and expertise in working with the media will form the core of our public representatives. But, we are encouraging more psychiatrists to take advantage of opportunities of working with the media, to publicly represent the profession in its efforts on behalf of the mentally ill as well as the healthy population, and to support the essential concept of public education so that both psychiatry and the public will benefit.

References

Colford, P.D. (1985, September 29). The talking cure. *Newsday,* part II, V, 4-5.

From deadlines to headlines: A guide to working with the news media. The University of Texas System Cancer Center, Department of Public Information and Education.

The Group for the Advancement of Psychiatry. (1982). *The child and television drama: The psychosocial impact of cumulative viewing* (Vol. XI, No. 112, 117). New York: Mental Health Materials Center.

The Group for the Advancement of Psychiatry. (1986). *A family affair: Helping families cope with mental illness: A guide for the professions* (Vol. XII, No. 119). New York: Brunner/Mazel.

Joint Commission on Public Affairs. (1977). Guidelines for psychiatrists working with the communications media. *American Journal of Psychiatry, 134,* 609-611.

Kelly, J. (1978). *Magazine writing today.* New York: Writers Digest Books.

Literary market place. (1986). New York: R.R. Bowker.

McAbee, T.A., Cafferty, T.P. (1982). Television public service announcements as outreach for potential clients. *American Journal of Community Psychology, 10,* 723-738.

McAlister, A., Puska, P., Koskela, K., Pallonen, U., & Maccoby, N. (1980). Mass communication and community organization for public health education. *American Psychologist, 35,* 375-379.

Munoz, R.F., Glish, M., Soo-Hoo, T., & Robertson, J. (1982). The San Francisco Mood Survey Project: Preliminary work toward the prevention of depression. *American Journal of Community Psychology, 10,* 317-329.

Psychiatry, the press and the public. (1949). Washington: American Psychiatric Association.

Regier, D.A., Myers, J.K., Kramer, M., Robins, L.N., Blazer, D.G., Haugh, R.L., Eaton, W.W., Locke, B.Z. (1984). The NIMA Epidemiologic Catchment Area Program. *Archives of General Psychiatry, 41,* 934-942.

Ruben, H.L. (1986). Revelations of a radio psychiatrist. *Hospital and Community Psychiatry, 37,* 934-936.

Rubenstein, C. (1981, December). Who calls in? It's not the lonely crowd. *Psychology Today,* 89-90.

Schanie, C.F., & Sundel, M. (1978). A community mental health innovation in mass-media preventive education: The alternative project. *American Journal of Community Psychology, 6,* 573-581.

Srole, L., Langer, T.S., Michael, S.T., Opler, M.K. & Rennie, T.A.C. (1962). *Mental health in the metropolis: The Mid-Town Manhattan Study.* New York: McGraw-Hill.

Traub, J. (1985, January/February). The world according to Nielsen. *Channels,* 26.

Wood, J. (1986). The editor's wishbook. *Writers Digest, 66,* 4.

APPENDIX 1

Excerpts from *GUIDELINES FOR PSYCHIATRISTS WORKING WITH THE COMMUNICATIONS MEDIA*

These guidelines were approved by the Board of Trustees of the American Psychiatric Association at its February 19, 1977 meeting, upon recommendations of the Joint Commission on Public Affairs.

To reaffirm the American Psychiatric Association's long-standing policy of full, open and honest communications with the American people, the Joint Commission on Public Affairs has prepared the following guidelines to help psychiatrists deal more effectively with the public media.

Part I. Basic Principles of Open Communication

The American Psychiatric Association has an open policy with regard to the communications media. The Association encourages frank sharing of its business and concerns with bona fide representatives of the news media. Members are encouraged to cooperate with the reporters on all matters within the expertise and interests of the psychiatric profession.

Public Relations

Sound judgment, common sense and the *Principles of Medical Ethics with Annotations Especially Applicable to Psychiatry*[1] should dictate psychiatrists' relations with the communications media. No amount of publicity or public relations can counteract poor performance.

Psychiatrists are responsible for constantly evaluating their performance and that of the profession as a whole and for remembering that their actions reflect on the entire profession.

The promise of radical cures or boasting of extraordinary skill or success is considered unethical by the medical profession. Likewise, claiming expertise in broad social matters without proof or positive contributions to solutions can destroy public trust. It is not necessary to comment on every question from the press.

The Patient: Confidentiality or Privilege

Release of information about individual patients must be considered in a different light from open communication because of the issues of confidentiality. The APA Board of Trustees adopted a *Position Statement on Guidelines for Psychiatrists:* Problems in Confidentiality,[2] parts of which are quoted below:

> The welfare of the patient is the first concern of the psychiatrist, and from this concern derives the psychiatrist's obligation to protect the patient's privacy and maintain the confidentiality of his communications. When, however, circumstances compel the psychiatrist to impart information about a patient to others, it is to be done in strict accordance with legal requirements and procedures, ethical guidelines, good judgment, and common sense, and always with the welfare of the patient as the underlying consideration. (p. 1543)
>
> A psychiatrist should never reveal, except with proper authorization or, if necessary, under legal compulsion, for example, a court order, confidential information disclosed to him/her by a patient in the treatment process. Consultation with one's own legal counsel may be necessary. (p. 1545)
>
> *Spectacular public crimes.* In case of persons who have been under psychiatric treatment and who subsequently become involved in spectacular public crimes or whose condition may constitute a threat to the welfare of the community, the

> confidentiality of records (other than necessary for proper medical treatment) should still be maintained. (p. 1545)
>
> *After death.* After the death of a person who has been under psychiatric care, the pertinent principle of medical ethics cited above still applies. The confidentiality of the patient's communications should always be maintained except when the release of information is authorized by the proper person (i.e., next of kin, executor) or under proper legal compulsion. (p. 1545)

Other matters involving confidentiality have been discussed in another position statement.[3]

The Psychiatrist as Commentator

Although no guidelines or policies can be formulated that will cover all situations, the following precautions may be helpful:

- No individual can speak for the profession as a whole. Official statements are made only by the Trustees or those officers of the American Psychiatric Association empowered to do so. Among the 25,000 members, there is an immense variety of opinions about any controversial issue.
- If one is in doubt, one should make no comment at all.
- Comments, if any, should be made thoughtfully. The reporter should be told that a statement will be prepared and that he/she will be called back shortly. Restraint should be the guiding rule in all contacts with the press, radio and television. Understatement is usually more effective than excessive approval or denunciation.
- In major cases of national interest, the inquiry may be referred to the American Psychiatric Association Division of Public Affairs office in Washington, DC.
- Reports may be referred to pertinent published articles or monographs that deal with the issue under discussion.

- In no case should a comment be made that might reflect adversely on the competence or character of individuals directly involved in a particular situation, not because physicians should be mutually protective, but because all the facts cannot be known in such circumstances.
- Consultation with the county medical society or district branch officials is always wise.
- Some reporters, like much of the general public, do not realize that psychiatrists are physicians. They should be told to accurately identify psychiatrists as M.D. rather than Dr.

References

1. The principles of medical ethics with annotations especially applicable to psychiatry. *Am J Psychiatry 130*:1058–1064, 1973.
2. Position statement on guidelines for psychiatrists: problems in confidentiality. *Am J Psychiatry 126*:1543–1549, 1970.
3. Position statement on the confidentiality of medical research records. *Am J Psychiatry 130*:739, 1973.

Excerpts from *ADDENDUM TO PUBLIC AFFAIRS GUIDELINES*

(Adopted by Board of Trustees of the American Psychiatric Association, March 13, 1982).

Part III. Radio and Television

The American Psychiatric Association encourages the responsible participation of psychiatrists in radio and television programs for the purpose of educating the public about psychiatry, mental illness and related subjects; and to advise the public on appropriate sources of quality mental health care in the community.

APPENDIX 2

SAMPLE BRIEF ANSWERS TO COMMONLY ASKED QUESTIONS

In any interview, whether it is print or media, only one or two points can be readily absorbed. Regardless of the length or the intensity of the interview, you should always bear in mind the fact that frequently only a very small portion of the interview will be transmitted to the public. If you are to have the optimal effect on your audience, state the essential points you wish to make clearly and concisely at the appropriate times during the interview. You will leave your audience with the desired message.

Happiness and Unhappiness

What is mental health?

In addition to absence of mental illness, mental health is the ability to cope with life's ups and downs and to work, love and play successfully.

Who should see a psychiatrist?

Individuals suffering from a mental illness—experiencing their reality with anxiety or emotional problems they cannot handle alone.

Is mental illness hereditary?

Some forms of mental illness have been shown to run in families, although they are not directly inherited from parent to child.

Who gets depressed?

Anyone who suffers a major loss, great stress or has a strong family history of depression may become depressed. Sometimes depression may be due to organic factors, including the use of medications or other drugs.

What is a psychiatric consultation?

Having a complete evaluation by a psychiatrist.

How can I find a psychiatrist?

Ask your physician, a friend or relative, or contact local or state medical psychiatric society offices.

Do psychiatrists treat everyone with medication?

Many patients are treated with psychotherapy without medication.

How do you know if you're mourning or depressed?

If the symptoms of grieving do not remit during the several months following the loss, it is likely that the mourning is evolving into depression.

What is the difference between mental health practitioners?

Psychiatrists are physicians. Psychologists can have Ph.Ds or Master's Degrees. Social workers and psychiatric nurses can have Master's or Bachelor's degrees. Psychoanalysts can be from the ranks of any of the former, although, more frequently, they are psychiatrists.

What if I don't like my psychiatrist?

You should discuss it with your psychiatrist and consider seeking a second opinion or changing psychiatrists.

Relation of Mind and Body

Can emotional stress cause headaches?

Definitely. Tension headaches are quite common.

What is an eating disorder?

An eating disorder is a disturbance of appetite and/or body image. It may include binging or starving oneself with possible use of laxatives, purgatives or self-induced vomiting.

Are nightmares abnormal?

Nightmares can be normal, but they often occur in the face of stress or emotional upset.

Is the use of drugs and alcohol a mental illness?

The abuse of and/or addiction to alcohol and drugs is a mental illness.

Is alcoholism hereditary?

Alcoholism does run in some families. There is a hereditary predisposition; it is not directly inherited from parents.

Is epilepsy a mental illness?

Epilepsy is not a mental illness; it is a neurologic disease. Epileptic seizures can alter a person's thinking, feeling and behavior.

Who Goes for Help?

What are the signs of depression?

Feeling sad, blue, helpless, hopeless, worthless or guilty; wishing to die; having sleep or appetite disturbances are among the significant signs.

What is a serious suicide threat?

Every suicide threat must be taken seriously.

What is schizophrenia?

A major mental illness characterized primarily by disordered thinking with delusions and/or hallucinations.

What is anxiety, an anxiety attack?

Anxiety is an overwhelming sense of dread for no discernible reason. An anxiety or panic attack is characterized by shortness of breath, rapid heartbeat, perspiring, lightheadedness and a fear of fainting, having a heart attack, or dying.

When is being obsessive a mental illness?

When a person cannot control intrusive thoughts or ideas that interfere with his/her life.

What is "multiple personality?"

The expression of independent personalities in the same individual at different times.

What is the difference between normal fears and phobias?

Phobias are unrealistic, overwhelming fears of objects, activities, or situations that interfere with your life.

Are there medications for tics?

Yes, one should be evaluated by a neurologist before being referred to a psychiatrist.

What is pathological gambling?

A compulsive need to gamble and to continue to gamble, despite inevitable devastating loss and disruption of daily life.

What are psychosomatic illnesses?

Physical illnesses such as headaches, ulcers, hypertension, certain skin diseases or backaches precipitated or aggravated by emotional distress.

Can mental illness diagnoses harmfully label a patient?

Unfortunately, our society still stigmatizes people with emotional illness to some extent.

What Kind of Treatments Help?

What is the purpose of psychiatric hospitalization?

To treat emotional illness intensively in a safe and secure environment.

What are the different kinds of psychotropic medications?

Antianxiety agents, antidepressants, antipsychotics, antimanic agents, hypnotics and agents which deter substance abuse (Disulfiram, Hatrexone).

Does a dependency develop to medication?

Antianxiety agents and hypnotics can cause dependency.

What is tardive dyskinesia?

An adverse effect of treatment with antipsychotic agents characterized by involuntary movements of the lips and tongue, the extremities and the trunk.

What is ECT?

Electro convulsive therapy—using electric current to alter severe, life-threatening depression.

What is psychotherapy?

The use of frank conversation with a mental health professional with the aim to change pathologic thoughts, attitudes, behavior, or symptoms in a patient.

How long should therapy last?

Depending on the goals set by the patient, until he or she has been relieved from symptoms, is able to cope better with life's tasks and/or has gained a deeper understanding of the reasons for his/her behavior.

Does therapy help?

In most instances.

Which therapies are valid?

Depending on the problem, psychoanalysis, individual psychotherapy, family or couples therapy, group therapy, behavioral therapy, sexual dysfunction therapy, or hypnotherapy may be indicated.

What is hypnosis and its uses?

Using relaxation techniques and suggestions to tap into a person's unconscious to motivate change.

What is behavior therapy?

Various techniques for analyzing and changing behavior without necessarily looking at unconscious motivation.

What is family therapy, marital therapy?

Working with the family system or the couple to understand and evaluate problems which frequently result from disrupted communications and stressful intrafamilial conflicts.

What is group therapy?

A therapist and four to ten people meet regularly in a group to discuss their problems and help each other toward healthful change.

What is sex therapy?

Exploring and prescribing techniques to correct sexual dysfunction.

Should therapists give advice on radio and TV?

Therapists can educate and refer people using the media.

Love and Sex

What is love?

The physical, erotic, emotional and intellectual feelings that attract one to another.

What is the relationship between love and sex?

Sex and intimacy can occur without love, but it is often part of a normal love relationship between mature adults.

What has been the effect of the "sexual revolution"?

To enable people to understand, explore and enjoy the potentiation of their own sexuality.

What happens to once good marriages that go bad?

Good marriages go bad when trust, respect, communication and/or romance are disrupted.

How honest should one be in a relationship?

Honesty is a cornerstone of a good, enduring relationship, but must not be used to hurt the other person.

Does sex therapy help?

Yes, sex therapy enables individuals to correct sexual dysfunction.

What is sexual dysfunction in a man?

Impotency, premature or retarded climax, decreased sexual desire or excitement, or Don Juanism.

What are common sexual problems in a woman?

Decreased sexual desire, decreased sexual excitement, spasm of vaginal muscles, and orgasmic inability.

What is a fetish?

An object, part of the body or a piece of clothing that for a given individual is necessary for the achievement of orgasm.

Is homosexuality a mental illness?

Homosexuality is a sexual-orientation variant, not a mental illness.

What is perversion?

Desire for an abnormal sexual object or activity in order to achieve orgasm.

Is masturbation harmless as generally practiced by normal adults?

Yes.

Anger, Hatred and Violence

Does movie and TV violence increase violent behavior?

This is a controversial issue. A disturbed individual may become violent after watching movie or TV violence.

Does pornography affect behavior?

Not necessarily, but violent pornography can influence the behavior of disturbed individuals.

Do victims of violence need psychological help?

Most certainly: to deal with their feelings of anger, grief and sadness.

Does parental violence adversely affect child development?

It is indeed detrimental to normal childhood development.

What is the difference between normal anger and rage?

Rage is intense and often uncontrolled anger.

Do psychiatrists risk physical harm from patients?

Most patients are not violent. However, some paranoid, psychotic individuals have been known to act violently toward their psychiatrists.

Should psychiatrists be held responsible for the behavior of their patients?

No one can be held responsible for the behavior of another, but if a patient tells a psychiatrist he is going to harm himself or another, the psychiatrist must take steps to prevent such action.

What is the role of the psychiatrist in an insanity defense?

To evaluate whether, at the time the offense occurred, the individual was suffering from a mental illness that affected his ability to conform his behavior to the requirements of the law.

Should the insanity defense be abolished?

The insanity defense is necessary to protect severely disturbed individuals from being punished for actions over which they had no control.

Children and Adolescents

What problems signal the need for psychiatric evaluation?

Major changes in behavior, e.g., in social and work relationships, in school behavior, in eating or sleeping patterns interfering with the individual's mental or physical health.

When should children learn "the facts of life?"

During preadolescence at the latest, children start asking questions. They should be given simple, straightforward answers.

What is the proper age to toilet train children?

From two to three years of age, (when the child is able to develop voluntary control).

Is spanking harmful to children?

It can be, and it is a poor way to control disapproved behavior. It is too often an undisciplined expression of parental exasperation.

Is child abuse increasing?

We have become increasingly aware of it as a society in the last decade.

How common is incest?

Much more common than we previously thought it to be.

Why do children and adolescents commit suicide?

There is no one cause. Possible reasons include the feeling of being unwanted and unloved, depression, behavioral problems, guilt, and substance abuse. When young people are depressed and hopeless, their relationships with parents and friends are impaired.

How close in age should siblings be?

Separating children by at least two to three years makes it easier for the older child to relinquish his position as the baby and welcome the implicit pleasures of peer companionship.

Is playing hookey from school a psychiatric problem?

It is a behavioral problem that can indicate underlying emotional problems.

Do foods cause hyperactivity in children?

There is some documented proof that they do, although some physicians are not convinced.

How can children be helped through a divorce?

Through self-help groups, group therapy, family or individual therapy, being persuaded they are loved and are not causative in the breakup.

What are the problems of stepparents?

Establishing an open, honest, loving relationship with the stepchildren; coping with conflictual attitudes of children's natural relatives.

Why do adolescents (children) use drugs?

They are exploring the limits of their own identity, frequently acting out against their parents, or reacting to peer pressure.

Why are some adolescents attracted to cults?

As a way to establish their identity and fulfill an overwhelming need for security and acceptance that they are not finding in their family and because cult leaders are skilled in seductive appeals to youths' perplexity and search for the security of certainty.

Should sex education be taught in school?

Most certainly, so that children can understand the facts and myths of sexual function and act responsibly, and because many parents are, through ignorance, inhibition, and their own painful mistakes, rendered inarticulate and unqualified to teach what their children need to guide them.

Is adolescent rebellion a "normal" phase?

During adolescence, children must separate from parents and create their own identity as individuals; this tends to take the form of adolescent rebellion.

What may cause problems for an adoptive child?

Establishing a sense of identity in the adoptive family with the knowledge that his family of origin could not or would not raise him.

Why do young girls or boys run away from home?

This is an act of rebellion that occurs in the context of a disrupted relationship within family.

What is anorexia nervosa?

An eating disorder affecting predominantly young women, characterized by a distorted sense of being fat, leading to self-starvation.

Older People

How common is depression in the elderly?

About three times as common as in the population in general.

How common is suicide in the elderly?

The elderly have the highest suicide rate of any segment of the population.

What are some common problems of retirement?

Boredom, financial problems, loss of feeling productive, needed, attractive and loved, unwillingness to accept waning physical powers and sometimes necessary dependence on the caring of others.

Is senility inevitable?

No.

What is Alzheimer's Disease?

A degenerative brain disease causing memory, thought and behavioral disturbances. It affects about 15 percent of persons over 65.

Ethics of Psychiatrists

Is a therapist's sexual relation with patients common in psychiatry?

It is medically unethical and has no therapeutic value. Unfortunately, sexual involvement occurs occasionally in professional relationships involving trust and intimate disclosure such as cast with lawyers, physicians, clergymen, etc.

Do psychiatrists advocate sexual permissiveness?

No.

Should an ethical psychiatrist treat family, friends?

A psychiatrist should not treat family members. As a general rule, it is inadvisable to treat friends, but it can be done within limits and is ethical. A personal relationship makes it difficult to have an appropriate therapeutic relationship.

What is confidential in psychiatric treatment?

Everything that the patient tells the psychiatrist, except for the psychiatrist's duty to warn or intervene if the patient is imminently dangerous to self or others.

Should psychiatrists inform the public of fraudulent treatments?

Most assuredly.

Is psychiatry used unethically in other countries?

Unfortunately, psychiatry is reportedly often abused for political control in certain countries with authoritarian governments.

Rights of Patients

Do psychiatric patients have the legal right to refuse treatment?

Yes, unless they have been certified by the courts as unable to appropriately judge what is important for their own safety or the safety of others.

What is deinstitutionalization?

The release of patients from large custodial psychiatric institutions with the goal of their becoming integrated into the least restrictive environment, preferably into a social network such as family, friends and community.

What changes are needed in the care of the mentally ill?

Increased availability of appropriate and affordable resources for care regardless of a person's ability to pay.

Why does psychiatry have such a poor public image?

The stigma and horror of mental illness has often been extended from the patients to those who treat them. Mental illness is frightening and people defend themselves against their fears by making fun of it and of those who treat it. Until recently psychiatrists have been little concerned with their public image. They have tried to remain in the background. Psychiatrists realize now that they can enhance their capacity to serve human needs by informing the public and by dispelling the myths about mental illness.

What is the stigma of mental illness?

There is more than one. The belief held by some is that mental illness represents moral weakness. It is also thought by some that all mentally ill people are crazy, violent, never get better, cannot work or be trusted, and are the burdensome dregs of humanity to be shunned and locked out of sight.

What is preventive psychiatry?

Preventing emotional illness before it occurs or providing the earliest possible treatment to lessen disability or the likelihood of recurrence.

APPENDIX 3

FACT SHEETS*

The following Fact Sheets provide useful background material about the major psychiatric conditions. They contain concise and simplified data and statistics which can be of use when being interviewed.

Facts About: Anxiety Disorders

- Anxiety disorders afflict *more than 13.1 million or 8.3 percent of Americans* and are the most common mental illnesses. Their symptoms can be so severe that victims are almost totally disabled. Anxiety is defined as a sense of irrational dread or fear. It is feeling more nervous than a situation calls for.
- The term "anxiety disorders" describes many disorders. Three major types of disorders are *phobias, panic disorders, and obsessive-compulsive disorders.*
- *Phobias afflict 11.1 million Americans or 7 percent of the population.*

  — People with phobias feel *terror, dread or panic* when confronted with the feared object, situation or activity. Many have so

*These Fact Sheets are reprinted with the permission and courtesy of the Division of Public Affairs and the Joint Commission on Public Affairs of the American Psychiatric Association. For updated copies of the Fact Sheets contact the Division of Public Affairs, American Psychiatric Association, 1400 K Street, NW, Washington, DC 20001.

overwhelming a desire to avoid the source of such fear that it interferes with their jobs, family life, and social relationships.
- Agoraphobia, the fear of being alone or in a public place that has no escape hatch (such as on a public bus), is *the most disabling* because victims can become housebound. The disease begins in late childhood or early adolescence and, left untreated, worsens with time.
- Social phobias are *fears of situations in which the victim can be watched* by others, such as public speaking, or in which the victim's behavior might prove embarrassing, such as eating in public. They begin in late childhood or early adolescence.
- Simple phobias are *fears of specific objects or situations* that cause terror similar to panic attacks. They can begin at any age. Examples are fear of snakes, fear of flying, fear of closed spaces.

• *Panic disorders afflict 1.2 million Americans.*

  - Victims suddenly suffer intense, *overwhelming terror for no apparent reason.* The fear is accompanied by heart palpitations, chest pain, sweating, faintness and trembling.
  - Sufferers *can't predict when the attacks will occur,* though certain situations such as driving a car can become associated with them.
  - Untreated, panic sufferers can despair and become suicidal.

• *Obsessive-compulsive disorders afflict 2.4 million Americans.* Victims attempt to cope with their anxiety by associating it with repeated, unwanted thoughts or ritual behaviors that themselves get out of control.

  - *Obsession victims are plagued with involuntary, recurrent and persistent thoughts* or impulses that are distasteful to them. Examples are thoughts of violence, or of becoming infected by shaking hands with others.
  - *People with compulsions go through repeated and involuntary ritualistic behaviors* that are supposed to prevent or produce a future

event, even though the behaviors themselves have nothing to do with that event. Examples are constantly washing hands or touching a particular object.
- *The disorders are often linked,* such as obsessions over infection and compulsive handwashing.
- Obsessive-compulsive disorders often begin in adolescence or early adulthood, generally are chronic and *cause moderate to severe impairment.*

- Anxiety disorders are treated by a combination approach. It is often useful to *gradually expose the patient* to the feared object or situation under controlled circumstances. *Medications can help* reduce the acute symptoms. In addition to behavioral modification techniques and medication, talking issues out in psychotherapy can be crucial. There is good reason for optimism about treatment of even the most severe anxiety disorder.

Facts About: Childhood Disorders

- *Emotional and developmental problems afflict 12 million children under the age of 18.* Untreated, the disorders can seriously impair the youngsters' emotional and intellectual development and may lead to chronic, lifelong mental illness.

  - Between *4 percent and 15 percent of these children receive any kind of treatment* through the mental health system. In comparison, 74 percent of the 7.6 millon physically handicapped youngsters receive care.
  - Childhood disorders affect not only the sufferer but his or her family and can lead to serious family problems that also require professional help.

- *Children of any age from preschoolers to older teenagers, can suffer from depression.* Like depressed adults, their symptoms are:

  1. *Feelings of sadness, hopelessness, worthlessness, low self-esteem and excessive guilt.*

2. *Loss of interest* in activities they once enjoyed.
3. Loss of energy, *fatigue;* inability to concentrate, noticeable *change in appetite and sleeping patterns.*
4. Recurring *thoughts of death* or suicide.

– *Suicide is the third leading cause of death among young people* and has more than tripled among teenagers in the last 20 years.
– *Every day, 18 young people commit suicide.* Every hour, 57 children and teenagers attempt to kill themselves.

- Disorders that specifically develop in childhood are placed into four general categories: Hyperkinetic behavioral or attention deficit disorders, pervasive developmental disorders, attachment disorders, and conduct disorders.
- *Hyperkinetic and attention deficit disorders* have many names: hyperactivity, minimal brain dysfunction, brain damage syndrome, and hyperkinetic syndrome.

– The disorder is *more common in boys than girls.* Though it often develops before the child is seven, it is most often recognized when the child is between the ages of eight and ten, after symptoms have gone on for at least six months.
– At that age, the child's *symptoms* are:

1. *Inability to finish any activity* that requires concentration, either at school or at home or play; shifts excessively from one activity to another.
2. Doesn't seem to listen.
3. Acts before thinking; *excessive activity;* runs or climbs excessively; fidgets excessively; moves excessively during sleep.
4. *Requires close supervision;* frequently calls out in class; has serious difficulty waiting his turn in games or group situations.

– Treatment often consists of *special educational programs* with small, structured classes, *support groups for family members,* and individual *psychotherapy.* In addition, *medications* such as amphetamines and methylphenidate help in reducing the hyperactive symptoms.

- Though quite rate, *pervasive developmental disorders* can afflict children as young as a few months of age. The term "pervasive developmental disorder" is used rather than "psychosis" because the *illnesses severely affect many basic areas of psychological development* that are needed for language and social skills.

  – *Infantile autism, which afflicts 200,000 children, develops before 30 months of age.*

    1. It is three times more common in boys than girls and it is 50 times more common in siblings of its victims than in the general population.
    2. As infants, they *don't respond to others and don't cuddle or look at their caregiver.* The child may have an aversion to affection or cling tenaciously to only one specific individual.
    3. As children, they are grossly impaired in communication skills. They either *never learn to talk* or, if they can talk, have *very peculiar speech patterns,* say "you" when they mean "I," and cannot name objects they know.
    4. They have *very bizarre reactions to their environment.* They can't adapt to minor changes in their environment such as a new place at the dinner table. They may become attached to strange objects, such as a rubber band or piece of string.
    5. The child may go through *ritualistic behavior,* such as hand clapping or other body movements.

- *Attachment disorders result from severe emotional neglect.* Evident as early as a few months of age, these disorders' symptoms include failure to thrive, failure to smile or look at caregivers, inability to crawl at the appropriate age, weak cry, and poor muscle tone.
- *Conduct disorders afflict children of any age* and are characterized by a pattern of behavior that goes far beyond normal childhood mischief and pranks. The children consistently ignore rules that

are reasonable and age-appropriate, can be violent, may consistently lie or steal, and may repeatedly run away from home for no reason.

- *Attachment and conduct disorders can be effectively treated* with a variety of methods, including psychotherapy and family therapy, which help the child and his or her family understand the illness and ways of coping with it.

Facts About: Depression

- *Depression afflicts 9.4 million people* or as many as two of ten Amerians.
- *Suicide,* the most serious result of depression, is the tenth leading cause of death in America and the *third leading cause of death among those aged 15 to 24.*

  – Every day, 18 teenagers kill themselves.
  – *Every hour 57 children and teenagers attempt to kill themselves.*

- Though the term "depression" can describe a normal human emotion, it also is the name of *a disease in which victims' moods are seriously disturbed* for at least two weeks and which can lead to serious disability and death.

  – In addition to *feelings of sadness, hopelessness and irritability,* depression includes at least four of these symptoms:

    1. Noticeable *change of appetite* with either significant weight loss when not dieting or weight gain.
    2. Noticeable *change in sleeping patterns,* such as fitful sleep, inability to sleep, or sleeping too much.
    3. *Loss of interest* in activities formerly enjoyed.
    4. Loss of energy; *fatigue.*
    5. Feelings of *worthlessness;* feelings of inappropriate *guilt.*
    6. *Inability to concentrate* or think; indecisiveness.
    7. Recurring *thoughts of death or suicide;* wishing to die; attempting suicide.

- If depression is accompanied by *melancholia* (defined as overwhelming feelings of sadness and grief), the victim also will suffer from waking at least two hours earlier than normal in the morning, from feeling more depressed in the morning, and a significant slowing of motor skills.
- *A few severely depressed persons may develop disturbed thinking;* for example, they might think their bodies are rotting.
- Depression can *appear at any age,* even in infants. Scientists estimate that more than half of those who have had one episode of major depression will have another episode.
- Some victims of depression have episodes that are separated by several years and others suffer clusters of the disorder over a short period. Between episodes, they can function normally. However, 20 percent to 35 percent of the victims suffer chronic depression that prevents them from completely functioning normally.

• Victims of *manic-depressive disorder,* another category of depression, suffer from wild swings in mood. They *alternate between extreme elation and severe depression.*

- During the manic phase, they are *hyperactive* and become excessively involved in activities that probably will have painful consequences. *They talk very loudly and rapidly, abruptly changing from topic to topic.* They need less sleep and might *go for days without rest.* They may have excessively high self-esteem to the point that they develop grandiose delusions.
- Manic-depressive disorder generally *appears before the age of 30.*

• Between *80 percent and 90 percent of all depressed patients can be effectively treated.* Sadly, 66 percent to 80 percent of this disease's victims never seek help.

- The best treatment is often a *combination of psychotherapy and medications.* This produces better results than either used alone. Psychotherapy helps patients understand their disorder better and relieves the stresses that lead to or worsen symptoms. When indicated, medications relieve symptoms and help patients function.

– *Manic-depression is effectively treated with Lithium,* which reduces the mania and augments psychotherapy.

Facts About: Manic-Depression

Manic-depressive illness, known in medical communities as *bipolar illness,* is the most distinct and dramatic of the depressive or affective disorders. Unlike major depression, which can occur at any age, manic-depressive illness generally strikes before the age of 30. Nearly one in 100 people will suffer from the disorder at some time in his or her life.

The distinction between bipolar illness and other depressive disorders is that patients swing from depression to mania, generally with periods of normal moods in between the two extremes. Some patients, however, cycle from mania to depression and back within a few days and without a period of normal mood. People with this condition are called "rapid cyclers."

Symptoms

When patients suffer a manic phase, they feel a rather sudden onset of elation or euphoria that increases in a matter of days to a serious impairment. Symptoms of the manic phase are:

- *A mood that is excessively good, euphoric or expansive.* The patient feels "on top of the world," and nothing—bad news, horrifying event, or tragedy—will change his or her happiness. The mood is way out of bounds, given the individual's personality.
- Expressions of *unwarranted optimism* and lack of judgment. Self-confidence reaches the point of *grandiose delusions* in which the person thinks he has a special connection with God, celebrities or political leaders. Or he may think that nothing—not even the laws of gravity—can stop him from accomplishing any task. As a

result, he may think he can step off a building or out of a moving car without being hurt.

- *Hyperactivity and excessive plans or participation in numerous activities that have a good chance for painful results.* He becomes so enthusiastic about activities or involvements that he fails to recognize he hasn't enough time in the day for all of them. For example, he may book several meetings, parties, deadlines and other activities in a single day, thinking he can make all of them on time. Added to the expansive mood, this can also result in reckless driving, spending sprees, foolish business investments, or sexual behavior unusual for the person.
- *Flight of ideas.* The person's thoughts race uncontrollably, like a car without brakes careening down a mountain. When the person talks, his words come out in a nonstop rush of ideas that abruptly change from topic to topic. In its severe form, the loud, rapid *speech becomes hard to interpret* because the patient's thought processes become so totally *disorganized and incoherent.*
- Decreased need for sleep, allowing the patient to go with *little or no sleep for days* without feeling tired.
- *Distractibility* in which the patient's attention is easily diverted to inconsequential or unimportant details.
- At times, the patient will become *suddenly irritable, enraged or paranoid* when his grandiose plans are thwarted or his excessive social overtures are refused.

Untreated, the manic phase can last as long as three months. As it abates, the patient may have a period of normal mood and behavior. But eventually the depressive phase of the illness will set in. This phase has the same symptoms as major or unipolar depression.

- Feelings of worthlessness, hopelessness, helplessness, total indifference and/or inappropriate guilt; prolonged sadness or unexplained crying spells; jumpiness or irritability, withdrawal from formerly enjoyable activities, social contacts, work or sex.
- Inability to concentrate or remember details.
- Loss of appetite or noticeable increase in appetite; persistent

fatigue and lethargy, insomnia or noticeable increase in the amount of sleep needed.
- Aches and pains, constipation, or other physical ailments that cannot be otherwise explained.

Theories About Causes

Medical research has hinted that the risk for depressive illnesses runs in families. Studies have indicated that close relatives of people suffering from bipolar illness are 10 to 20 times more likely to develop either depression or manic-depressive illness than the general population. In fact, between 80 percent and 90 percent of people suffering from manic-depressive disorder have relatives who suffer from some form of depression. If one parent suffers from manic-depressive illness, a child has a 30 percent risk for suffering from a depressive disorder; if both parents suffer from manic-depressive illness, the children have a 75 percent chance of developing a depressive disorder.

No single gene has been linked to the disorders.* Possibly, people inherit a vulnerability to manic-depressive illness that is triggered by environmental factors or other causes. Comprehensive psychoanalytic studies indicate manic-depressive people were reared to become achievers in order to bring honor to their families; however, at the same time, they were never allowed to become fully autonomous. The research suggests that these people grow up with a need to achieve and a contradictory need to depend on others. Failure to reach a goal or to maintain a needed relationship triggers the manic-depressive illness.

Other studies suggest that imbalances in the biochemistry that controls a person's mood could contribute to manic-depressive illness. For example, people suffering from either manic-depressive or major depressive disorders often respond to certain hormones or steroids in a way that indicates they have irregularities in their

*More recent research has revealed DNA sequences apparently related to manic/depressive illness located on certain genes.

hormone production and release. Others hint that bipolar patients' neurotransmitters—chemicals by which brain cells communicate—become imbalanced during various phases of the disease. Finally, some people suffering from depressive illnesses have sleep patterns in which the dream phase begins earlier in the night than normal. These studies indicate that manic-depressive illness and major depression may be caused by biochemical imbalances. They help develop scientific theories about how medications work and hold hope that psychiatrists will someday be able to use laboratory tests to identify unipolar or bipolar illnesses.

Treatment

Many other physical and mental disorders can mimic manic-depressive illnesses. For example, a person with symptoms of manic-depression could be reacting to substances such as amphetamines or steroids or could suffer from an illness such as multiple sclerosis. Anyone who has symptoms of bipolar disorder should receive a thorough medical evaluation to rule out any other mental or physical disorders and to ensure accurate diagnosis and treatment.

Though manic-depressive disorder can become disabling, it is also among the most treatable of the mental illnesses. The combination of psychotherapy and medications returns the vast majority of manic-depressive patients to happy, functioning lives.

The most common medication, lithium carbonate, successfully reduces the number and intensity of manic episodes for 70 percent of those who take the medication. Twenty percent become completely free of symptoms. Those who respond to lithium best are patients who have a family history of depressive illness and who have periods of relatively normal mood between their manic and depressive phases.

Very effective in treating the manic phase, lithium also appears to prevent repeated episodes of depression. One theory for this is that in controlling the mania, lithium helps prevent the swing into depression. Lithium works by bringing various neurotransmitters in the brain into balance. Scientists think the medication may affect the way or the speed at which brain cells break down the neurotransmitters that are thought to control moods.

However, like all medications, lithium can have *side effects and must be very closely monitored by a psychiatrist.* The doctor should measure the level of lithium in the patient's blood as well as how well the patient's kidneys and thyroid gland are working. Among the side effects are weight gain, excessive thirst and urination, stomach and intestinal irritation, hand tremors, and muscular weakness. More serious side effects are hypothyroidism, kidney damage, confusion, delirium, seizures, coma and, in patients who aren't closely monitored by a physician, even death.

Properly monitored, however, lithium has returned thousands of people to happy, functioning lives that would not be possible without medication. The complications of this disorder include financial, social, family and occupational disintegration, and suicide.

Generally, people in treatment for manic-depressive illness also receive psychotherapy. Like all serious illnesses, manic-depressive disorders disrupt a person's relationships with others, self-esteem, and self-image. Medications can control the symptoms, but patients often also need to work out the side effects of the illness and to live with their new range of emotions. This is where psychotherapy is useful. With the help of the therapist, the patient can work out the problems created by the disorder and reestablish the relationships and healthy self-image that are shaken by the illness. In many cases, a patient needs the therapist's support to ensure that he or she complies with treatment.

Bibliography for Manic-Depressive Illness

Burch, C. (1972). *Stranger in the family: A guide to living with the emotionally disturbed.* Indianapolis: Bobbs-Merrill.

Corfman, E. (1979). *Depression, Manic Depressive Illness, and Biological Rhythms* (Science Reports). National Institute of Mental Health, Department of Health and Human Services Public Health Service; Alcohol, Drug Abuse and Mental Health Administration, 5600 Fishers Lane, Rockville, MD 20857.

Greist, J., & Jefferson, J.W. (1984). *Depression and its treatment: Help for the nation's #1 mental problem.* Washington, DC: American Psychiatric Press.

Korpell, H.S. (1984). *How you can help: A guide for families of psychiatric hospital patients.* Washington, DC: American Psychiatric Press.

Park, C.C., & Shapiro, L.N. (1976). *You are not alone: Understanding and dealing with mental illness—A guide for patients, families, doctors and other professionals.* Boston: Little Brown.

Winokur, G., Clayton, P.J., & Reich, T. (1969). *Manic depressive illness.* St. Louis: C.V. Mosby.

National Institute of Mental Health, Division of Communications, 5600 Fishers Lane, Rockville, MD 20857.

National Depressive and Manic Depressive Association, P.O. Box 753, Northbrook, IL 60062.

National Alliance for the Mentally Ill, 1200 Fifteenth Street, NW, Suite 400, Washington, DC 20005.

National Mental Health Association, 1021 Prince Street, Alexandria, VA 22314.

Facts About: Mental Health of the Elderly

Having good mental health throughout life does not provide immunity from severe depression, Alzheimer's disease, anxiety disorders, and other disorders after retirement. In fact, some studies show elderly people are at greater risk for mental disorders and their complications than are younger Americans.

- Between 15 percent and 25 percent of the elderly suffer from significant symptoms of mental illness.
- The highest suicide rate in America is among those aged 50 and older. This age group represents 26 percent of the total US population, but accounts for 39 percent of the suicides nationwide. That means 8,500 older Americans kill themselves each year.
- The elderly lead the World Health Organization's list of new cases of mental illness: 236 elderly per 100,000 suffer from mental illness, compared to 93 per 100,000 for the next younger group.
- Severe organic brain disorders afflict one million elderly, and mild to moderate organic brain disorders afflict another two million elderly.

Sadly, the elderly are unlikely to seek psychiatric treatment, which could cure or alleviate their symptoms and return them to their previous level of functioning. Why? Many older people don't understand mental illness or acknowledge that it even exists. Medicare has traditionally discriminated against psychiatric care. Individuals, their loved ones and friends, and often their own doctors fail to recognize the symptoms of treatable mental illness in older people. They blame them on "old age." As a result:

- Though the elderly make up 12 percent of the population and nearly one-fourth suffer from symptoms of mental illness, only four percent of the patients in community mental health centers are elderly.
- Only two percent of the patients seen in private practitioners' offices or hospitals are elderly.
- Less than 1.5 percent of the direct costs for treatment of mental illness is spent on behalf of older people living in the community.

Mental illnesses can be diagnosed and treated. Don't ignore noticeable changes in an older person's behavior or moods. Seek medical and psychiatric evaluations which can lead to treatments that can return an older person to a productive and happy life.

Depression

Depression, considered the most common mental disorder, afflicts 20 percent of people aged 65 and older. That number may be too low. Because depression can mimic senility, researchers also estimate that between 20 percent and 30 percent of those diagnosed as senile actually suffer from depression that, if treated, is reversible.

If any of these symptoms of depression last for more than two weeks, you should seek help for yourself or an older loved one:

- Feelings of worthlessness, hopelessness, helplessness, total indifference and/or inappropriate guilt; prolonged sadness or unexplained crying spells; jumpiness or irritability; losing interest and withdrawing from formerly enjoyable activities, family, friends, work or sex.

- Unexplainable loss of memory or the ability to concentrate; confusion and disorientation.
- Thoughts of death or suicide; suicide attempts.
- Loss of appetite or a noticeable increase in appetite; persistent fatigue and lethargy; insomnia or a noticeable increase in the amount of sleep needed.
- Aches and pains, constipation, or other physical ailments that cannot be otherwise explained.

Dementias

Dementia, commonly called senility, certainly is not an inevitable part of growing old. In fact, only 15 percent of older Americans suffer from this condition. Of that number, an estimated 60 percent suffer from Alzheimer's disease, a progressive mental deterioration for which no cause or cure has been found. Another 20 percent are thought to result from blood vessel disease in the brain, and the other 20 percent are caused by other factors.

An estimated 40 percent of all dementias are caused by:

- Multi-infarct dementia, the medical term for the inaccurate but popular term "hardening of the arteries of the brain." Those with this form of dementia have a history of high blood pressure, blood vessel disease, or a previous stroke. Deterioration is in steps rather than progressive.
- Multiple sclerosis, which destroys the nerve cells' protective covering and causes both mental and physical deterioration over many years.
- Parkinson's disease, which generally begins with involuntary and small tremors or problems with voluntary movements. Dementia occurs when the disease is severe or very advanced.
- Huntington's disease, a genetic disorder that begins in middle age and has symptoms of changed personality, mental decline, psychosis, and movement disturbance.

- Creutzfeldt-Jakob disease, thought to be caused by viral infection that causes a rapid and progressive dementia.

In addition, drug interactions or overdoses, poor diet, and other physical or mental problems can also cause symptoms that mimic dementia. Depression most often mimics dementia because its victims withdraw, can't concentrate, and appear confused.

Because these pseudodementias can be reversed when their causes are diagnosed and treated, psychiatrists first provide a complete medical evaluation to differentiate true dementia from these other factors that could mimic the condition.

- *Drugs.* Elderly people take many more prescription and over-the-counter medications than other age groups. Because their metabolism is slower, these drugs can stay in the body longer and reach toxic levels more quickly. Moreover, because many older people take more than one drug and may drink alcoholic beverages, they have a much higher risk that the drugs will interact, causing confusion, mood changes, and other symptoms of dementia.
- *Chemical imbalances caused by poor nutrition.* Because the brain requires a steady supply of proper nutrients, poor eating habits or problems with digestion can upset the way the brain functions. For example, pernicious anemia, a blood disorder caused by inability to use B vitamins, cause irritability, depression or dementia. Too little sugar in the bloodstream also causes confusion and personality change.
- *Diseases of the heart or lungs.* The brain also requires a great deal of oxygen to work properly. If diseased lungs cannot draw enough oxygen into the blood or a diseased heart fails to pump enough blood to the brain, lack of oxygen can affect the brain and behavior.
- *Diseases of the adrenal, thyroid, pituitary or other glands* that help regulate emotions, perceptions, memory and thought processes.

Alzheimer's Disease

One form of dementia—Alzheimer's disease— has received increasing attention in the years since the German psychiatrist, Alois Alzheimer, first described it in 1907.

- Alzheimer's disease is the fourth leading cause of death in America. An adult's chances of developing the illness are one in 100. One million people over 65 are severely afflicted with Alzheimer's disease and another two million are moderately affected.
- The odds of developing Alzheimer's disease increases fourfold among family members of a person suffering from the disorder.
- The physical hallmarks of Alzheimer's disease are an abnormal number of changes both inside and outside the brain's nerve cells. These changes include an excess of:

  – Neurofibrillary tangles, which appear to be pieces of normal fibers within the brain cells that have become tangled around each other in the form of a helix.
  – Neuritic plaques, which are degenerating bits of nerve cells which surround a protein that normally is not found in the brain. These plaques are outside the brain cells.

Symptoms

- The onset of Alzheimer's disease is usually very slow and gradual. The first symptom is *loss of recent, short-term memory.* For example, a person forgets to turn off the stove or remember which medications he or she took that morning. Mild personality changes such as increased apathy or social withdrawal also occur.
- As the disease progresses, the patient has trouble with abstract thinking, working with numbers when paying bills, understanding what is being read, or in organizing his or her day. The

person also may become more irritable, agitated, quarrelsome, and less neat in appearance.
- In late stages of the disease, the patient becomes confused or disoriented about time and year and unable to describe where he or she lives or name a recently visited place. The person ultimately stops conversing, becomes erratic in mood and uncooperative, incontinent and, in extreme cases, unable to care for himself or herself.

Medical science doesn't know what causes Alzheimer's disease.* Researchers have learned that the brains of Alzheimer's disease patients have as much as 30 times the normal amount of aluminum in them; other studies have shown that patients' brains have inappropriate levels of the enzyme choline acetyltransferase, a brain chemical that is important in memory loss and disorientation. Other studies have looked at the possibility that a slow-acting virus causes the progressive brain damage seen in Alzheimer's disease. Though results of all this research continue to be promising, medical science still has not defined the cause of Alzheimer's disease. As a result, the cure remains elusive.

Bibliography for Mental Health of the Elderly

"Plain talk about aging." National Institute of Mental Health, Division of Communications and Education, 5600 Fishers Lane, Rockville, MD 20857.

"Fact Sheet: Depression in the Elderly." US Department of Health and Human Services, Public Health Service, Alcohol, Drug Abuse and Mental Health Administration, 5600 Fishers Lane, Rockville, MD 20857.

"The dementias: Hope through research." US Department of Health and Human Services, National Institutes of Health Publication No. 81-2252, March 1982. Sold through the Superintendent of Documents, U.S. Government Printing Office, Washington, DC 20402.

"Progress report on senile dementia of the Alzheimer's type," National Institute of Aging NIH Publication No. 81-2343, September 1981. US Department of Health and Human Services, National Institute on Aging Information Office, 5600 Fishers Lane, Rockville, MD 20857.

---

*Very recent research has discovered a genetic basis at least with some Alzheimer disease families who manifest autosomal dominant disease traits identified through a chromosomal defect.

Atkinson, R.M. (Ed.) (1984). *Alcohol and drug abuse in old age.* Washington, DC: American Psychiatric Press.

Group for the Advancement of Psychiatry. (in press). *The psychiatric treatment of Alzheimer's disease.* New York: Brunner/Mazel.

Hospital and Community Psychiatry Service. (1985). *The elderly mentally ill.* Washington, DC: American Psychiatric Press.

Mace, N.L. & Rabins, P.V. (1981). *The 36-hour day.* Baltimore, MD: Johns Hopkins University Press.

Powell, L. & Courtice, K. (1983). *Alzheimer's disease: A guide for families.* Reading, MA: Addison-Wesley.

Shamoian, C.A. (Ed.) (1985). *Treatment of affective disorders in the elderly.* Washington, DC: American Psychiatric Press.

Shamoian, C.A. (Ed.) (1985). *Biology and treatment of dementia in the elderly.* Washington, DC: American Psychiatric Press.

Stanley, B. (1985). *Geriatric psychiatry: Clinical, ethical and legal issues.* Washington, DC: American Psychiatric Press.

The Alzheimer's Disease and Related Disorders Association, 292 Madison Ave., New York, NY 10017.

American Geriatrics Society, 10 Columbus Circle, New York, NY 10019.

American Association of Retired Persons, 1909 K Street, NW, Washington, DC 20049.

National Council of Senior Citizens, 925 15th St., NW, Washington, DC 20005.

National Council on the Aging, 600 Maryland Ave., SW, West Wing 100, Washington, DC 20024.

National Institute on Aging, 9000 Rockville Pike, Building 31, Room 2C-02, Bethesda, MD 20205.

US Department of Health and Human Services, Administration on Aging, 330 Independence Ave., SW, Room 4759, Washington, DC 20201.

Facts About: Mental Illness

- *Mental illness is a disease.* Like physical diseases, a mental illness has nothing to do with personal strengths or weaknesses, will power, or morality. Just as other diseases have specific symptoms and treatment, mental illnesses can be accurately diagnosed and effectively treated.
- *Mental illness can strike anyone at any time.* At any given time, between 30 million and 45 million Americans—nearly one in five people—are suffering from some form of mental illness that requires professional treatment.

  — *12 million children* suffer from *autism, depression and other diseases* that, left untreated, interfere with normal development.

- *13 million Americans* suffer from *alcohol abuse* or dependence and another *12.5 million Americans* suffer from *drug abuse* or dependence.
- *1.5 million Americans* suffer from *schizophrenic disorders* and 300,000 new cases occur each year.
- Right now, *more than 9 million Americans* are suffering from *depression, manic-depression and other depressive disorders.* About 30 million people or 15 percent of the population will suffer from at least one episode of major depression during their lifetime.
- *Nearly one-fourth of the elderly* who are written off as senile actually *suffer mental illness* that can be effectively treated.

• *Mental illness afflicts men and women.* Studies by the US Alcohol, Drug Abuse and Mental Health Administration indicate men are more likely to suffer from drug and alcohol abuse and personality disorders, and women are at higher risk for suffering from depression and anxiety disorders. All these disorders can be effectively treated.

• *The personal and social costs of mental illnesses are similar to those for heart disease and cancer.*

- Direct costs of mental illness are estimated to be $20.9 billion a year.
- Direct costs of substance abuse disorders are estimated to be $109 billion a year.
- Added to indirect costs, the total cost of substance abuse disorders rises to between $185 billion and $190.6 billion a year.

• *Treatment is available, but only one in five people who have a mental illness seek help.*

- About half of those suffering from schizophrenia seek treatment. Medications effectively stop acute symptoms in 80 percent of all patients.

- Fewer than one-fourth of those suffering from anxiety disorders seek treatment. However, psychotherapy, behavior therapy, contextual therapy, and some medications effectively treat these illnesses.
- Fewer than one-third of those suffering from depressive disorders seek treatment. But with treatment, 80 percent to 90 percent of those who suffer from these diseases can get better.
- Tragically, only *4 percent to 15 percent of the children suffering serious mental illness receive appropriate treatment.*

Facts About: Post-Traumatic Stress Disorder

It's been called "shell shock," "battle fatigue," and "war neurosis." But the disorder is not limited to soldiers. In the past, it was often misunderstood or misdiagnosed. But the disorder has very specific symptoms that, taken together, form a definite psychological syndrome.

The disorder is called *post-traumatic stress disorder* (PTSD) and it affects hundreds of thousands of people who have survived the trauma of natural disasters such as earthquakes, accidental disasters such as airplane crashes, or deliberate, man-made disasters such as war.

Psychiatrists estimate that several hundred thousand of the 3.5 million men and women who served in the Vietnam War are affected by post-traumatic stress disorder. Still more show some symptoms of the disorder. Studies indicate that veterans of heavy combat are more likely to suffer from post-traumatic stress disorder. Not all people who experience trauma require treatment; some recover with the help of family, friends, pastor or rabbi. But many do need professional help to successfully recover from the psychological damage that can result from experiencing, witnessing, participating in an overwhelmingly traumatic event.

The Symptoms

Post-traumatic stress disorder rarely appears during the trauma itself. Though its symptoms can occur soon after the event, post-traumatic stress disorder often *surfaces several months or even years later.*

People suffering from this disorder have repeated episodes in which they *reexperience the traumatic event.* This can happen in sudden, vivid memories that are accompanied by very painful emotions and take over the victim's attention. The memory can be a *flashback*—a recollection that is so strong that the individual thinks he is actually experiencing the traumatic event again or seeing it unfold before his eyes.

When a person has a severe flashback, he or she is in a *dissociative state,* which sometimes can be mistaken for sleepwalking. When that happens, the person acts as if he were actually experiencing the traumatic event again. But he isn't fully conscious of what he is doing. For example, a war veteran may begin prowling around his or her neighborhood as if patrolling hostile territory.

At other times, the reexperience occurs in *nightmares* that are so powerful the person awakens screaming in terror, as if he were reenacting the trauma in sleep. As a result, people with post-traumatic stress disorder often develop *insomnia* in an attempt to avoid the dreaded dreams.

At times, the reexperience comes as a *sudden, painful onslaught of emotions* that seem to have no cause. These emotions are often of grief and bring tears and a tight throat, but can also be of anger or fear. Individuals say these emotional experiences occur repeatedly, much like memories or dreams about the traumatic event.

Another set of symptoms includes what are called *avoidance phenomena.* These affect the person's relationships with others, because he or she often avoids close emotional ties with family, colleagues and friends. At first, the person feels numb, has *diminished emotions and can complete only routine, mechanical activities.* Later, when reexperiencing the event begins, the individual alternates between the flood of emotions caused by reexperiencing and the inability to feel or express emotions at all. People who suffer post-traumatic stress disorder often say they can't feel emotions, especially toward those who are closest; if they can feel emotions, often they can't express them. As the avoidance continues, the person seems to be bored, cold or preoccupied. Family members often feel rebuffed by the person because he or she lacks affection and acts mechanically.

The person also *avoids situations that remind him of the traumatic event* because his symptoms worsen when he is in a situation or activity that resembles, even in part, the original trauma. For example, a person who survived a prisoner-of-war camp might overreact to seeing people wearing uniforms similar to those of the camp guards. Over time, the person can become so fearful of particular situations that his or her daily life is ruled by attempting to avoid them.

Others, particularly war veterans, *avoid accepting responsibility* for others because they think they failed in ensuring the safety of those killed or injured during battle. As a result of this, many with PTSD have poor work records, trouble with their bosses and poor relationships with their family and friends.

War veterans can *become suddenly irritable or explosive,* even when they aren't provoked. This may result from leftover feelings of exploitation by superiors during the war or anger over their helplessness as they waited for orders or fulfilled illogical orders.

Others with PTSD say they have trouble concentrating or remembering current information.

Some war veterans and others suffering the disorder are always on guard for danger. As a result, they have *exaggerated startle reactions.* War veterans may revert to their war behavior when they hear sounds, such as backfiring cars or fireworks, which are similar to common battle sounds. At times, those with PTSD may suffer panic attacks. These can result from the extreme fear they felt during the traumatic event which remained unresolved during later events in their lives. During the attack, their throats tighten, breathing and heart rate increase, and they feel dizzy and nauseated.

Many *feel guilty because they survived* the disaster when others—particularly friends or family—did not. In combat veterans, this guilt may be worse if they witnessed or participated in behavior that was necessary to survive but is unacceptable in society. Such guilt can contribute to depression as the individual begins to look on himself as unworthy, a failure, a person who violated his own pre-war values.

Depression also can stem from the patient's inability to work out his grief over the loss of friends or family during the traumatic event. As long as the individual cannot come to terms with the impact of the trauma, it may continue to control his behavior without his even being aware of it.

Finally, many who suffer post-traumatic stress disorder attempt to rid themselves of their painful reexperiences, loneliness, and panic attacks by using *alcohol or other drugs as a "self-medication"* that helps them blunt their emotions and forget the trauma.

Treatments

Despite the very painful and real effects of post-traumatic stress disorder, the condition can be successfully treated. Using a variety of methods, psychiatrists and other mental health professionals help individuals work through the trauma and pain to resolve the resulting grief which they often could not even express.

Among the treatments is *individual psychotherapy.* Post-traumatic stress disorder results, in part, from the difference between the individual's personal values or view of the world and the reality that he or she witnessed or lived during the traumatic event. Psychotherapy, then, focuses on helping the individual examine his values and how his behavior and experience during the traumatic event violated them. The goal is resolution of the conscious and unconscious conflicts that were thus created. In addition, the individual works to build his self-esteem and self-control, develops a good and reasonable sense of personal accountability and renews his sense of integrity and personal pride.

In addition, therapists may recommend *family therapy* because spouses' and children's behaviors may result from and affect the individual suffering post-traumatic stress disorder. Spouses and children report their loved one doesn't communicate, show affection, or share in family life. By working with the family, the therapist can help to bring about change within the family. Its members can learn to recognize and cope with the range of emotions each feels. They do this by learning good communication, parenting and stress management techniques.

Rap groups are another effective treatment for many suffering post-traumatic stress disorder. This method encourages survivors of similar traumatic events to share their experiences and reactions to them. In doing so, group members help each other realize that many people would have done the same thing and felt the same emotions. That, in turn, helps the individual realize that he is not uniquely unworthy or guilty. Over time, the individual changes his opinion of himself and others and can build a new view of the world and redefine a positive sense of self.

Generally, such treatments can be completed on an outpatient basis. But if the disorder is so severe that the person is dangerous to himself or others, inpatient treatment might be recommended.

Facts About: Schizophrenia

- Schizophrenia is a term used to describe a complex condition that *afflicts 1.5 million Americans* and accounts for 40 percent of all days in institutional, long-term care. By comparison, heart disease accounts for 27 percent of long-term care days.
- *Everyone has a 1 in 100 chance of developing the disease.* Children of those suffering from schizophrenia have a 1 in 10 chance of developing the disease. This year, 300,000 new cases will develop.
- Research indicates that *there may be a biological basis for schizophrenia.* Studies show a possible link between schizophrenia and either too much or too little of various brain chemicals. Other studies indicate that brains of persons with schizophrenia may differ in structure or metabolism from healthy people.
- Schizophrenia begins gradually, creating inner turmoil in its victims. *The symptoms worsen to become severe distortions in perception, speech and thoughts.* Among the symptoms:

  - *Paranoid delusions,* which are unshakable thoughts that convince the victims that others are plotting against them.
  - Delusions that their *thoughts are "broadcast"* outside their head so others can hear them.
  - Delusions that *outside forces are controlling thoughts,* inserting them into the victim's head or removing them from the victim's mind.

- Hallucinations in which *voices threaten, insult or command the victim.* Less common hallucinations affect the other senses, such as seeing nonexistent things.
- *Emotions are blunted or inappropriate* to the situation, such as laughing at sad events.
- Like many physical diseases, *schizophrenia's symptoms come and go,* and its victims have periods when they can function normally. Chronic schizophrenia, however, is a progressive deterioration of the mental processes.

• Schizophrenia almost always *begins in adolescence or early adulthood.* Some victims suffer only one episode, while others suffer repeated episodes throughout their lives.
• Treatment generally *combines therapies* because the disease is so complex.

- *Antipsychotic medications* usually relieve the hallucinations and delusions.
- *Psychotherapy* helps victims understand their disease and assists in learning to distinguish reality from distorted perceptions. *Family therapy* helps spouses, parents or siblings learn about the disease and helps the patient live in the community. Because schizophrenia develops when victims are beginning careers or new social and family lives, the chronically ill also may need *rehabilitation, occupational and vocational therapy* so they can master daily living tasks, social interaction and job skills.

• Much of the *progress in treating schizophrenia results from medications.* Fifty-five percent of schizophrenia victims who do not take medications will suffer a relapse within two years of being discharged from a psychiatric facility. That compares to a relapse rate of 20 percent for victims who do take medications.
• Though science has not yet found a single cure, *schizophrenia can be effectively treated.* One long-term study of almost 2,000 patients found that 25 percent fully recovered, half recovered partially, and 25 percent required lifelong care.

Facts About: Substance Abuse

- *Alcohol and drug abuse afflicts 25.5 million Americans.* When its effect on the abusers' families and people close to those injured or killed by intoxicated drivers are included, such abuse affects an additional 40 million people.
- *Alcoholism costs a total of $89.5 billion* for treatment and indirect losses such as reduced worker productivity, early death, and property damage resulting from alcohol-related accidents and crime each year. *Drug abuse drains a total of $46.9 billion* in direct and indirect costs to business and the economy.
- *Substance abuse* victims can't control their use of alcohol or other drugs. They become intoxicated on a regular basis (daily, every weekend, or in binges) and often *need the drug for normal daily functioning.* They repeatedly *try to stop using the drug but fail,* even when they know the drug causes or worsens a physical ailment. Use of the drug interferes with their family life, social relationships, and work performance.
- *Substance dependence* victims suffer all the symptoms of abuse plus a tolerance for the drug so that *increased amounts of it are necessary* for the desired effects. Opioids, alcohol and amphetamines also lead to physical dependence in which the person develops withdrawal symptoms when he or she stops using the drug.
- *Ten million adults and three million children are alcoholics.* These people will die 10 years earlier than nonalcoholics.
- *Alcoholic drivers kill 28,000* people in traffic accidents each year.
- Alcoholism is a *progressive disease* that generally first appears between the ages of 20 and 40, though *children can become alcoholic.*

  — It takes 5 to 15 years of heavy drinking for an adult to become alcoholic; *it takes 6 to 18 months of heavy drinking for an adolescent to become alcoholic.*

  — Generally, *abuse occurs in one of three patterns:* regular, daily intoxication; drinking large amounts of alcohol at specific times, such as every weekend; and long periods of sobriety interspersed with binges of heavy daily drinking that last for weeks or months.

- As drinking continues, *dependence develops and sobriety brings serious withdrawal symptoms* such as delirium tremens (DTs) which include physical trembling, delusions, hallucinations, sweating and high blood pressure.
- *Long-term, heavy drinking can cause dementia,* in which the individual loses his memory, the ability to think abstractly, to recall names of common objects, to use correct words to describe recognized objects or to follow simple instructions.

- *Drug abuse afflicts more than 12.5 million Americans.* Of these, seven million use addictive prescription drugs without physician supervision, five million abuse cocaine, and a half million are addicted to heroin.
- The five major classes of drugs are sedative-hypnotics, opiates, hallucinogens, marijuana, and psychostimulants. Not all are physically addictive, but all can lead to psychological addiction in which the user needs the drug in order to function.

  - Abuse of *sedative-hypnotics or barbiturates* most often begins either as a prescription for insomnia among middle-class women between 30 and 60, or as a recreational experiment among men in their teens or early 20s. Often, abusers regularly take heavy daily doses and develop an addiction.
  - Abuse of *opioids such as heroin or morphine* generally follows abuse of other drugs such as alcohol, marijuana, sedatives, hallucinogens or amphetamines. About half of those who abuse the drugs develop a dependence or addiction.

- Successful treatment of drug and alcohol abuse includes a variety of therapies *geared toward abstinence.*

  - Psychotherapy helps the patients understand their behavior and motivations, develop higher self-esteem, and cope with stress. Self-help groups such as Alcoholics Anonymous also are effective.
  - The only medication for alcoholism requires daily use of dis-

ulfiram (Antabuse), which induces violent physical reactions to alcohol.

– Opiate addicts have been treated with methadone, a long-acting medication that maintains tolerance to opiates but substantially reduces the positive effects of heroin. Another treatment relies on opiate antagonists, which block the effect of the abused drug.

GAP COMMITTEES AND MEMBERSHIP

COMMITTEE ON ADOLESCENCE
Clarice J. Kestenbaum, New York, N.Y., Chairperson
Hector R. Bird, New York, N.Y.
Ian A. Canino, New York, N.Y.
Warren J. Gadpaille, Denver, Colo.
Michael G. Kalogerakis, New York, N.Y.
Silvio J. Onesti, Jr., Belmont, Mass.

COMMITTEE ON AGING
Gene D. Cohen, Washington, D.C., Chairperson
Eric D. Caine, Rochester, N.Y.
Charles M. Gaitz, Houston, Tex.
Gabe J. Maletta, Minneapolis, Minn.
Robert J. Nathan, Philadelphia, Pa.
George H. Pollock, Chicago, Ill.
Kenneth M. Sakauye, Chicago, Ill.
Charles A. Shamoian, Larchmont, N.Y.
F. Conyers Thompson, Jr., Atlanta, Ga.

COMMITTEE ON ALCOHOLISM AND THE ADDICTIONS
Edward J. Khantzian, Haverhill, Mass., Chairperson
Richard J. Frances, Newark, N.J.
Sheldon I. Miller, Newark, N.J.
Robert B. Millman, New York, N.Y.
Steven M. Mirin, Westwood, Mass.
Edgar P. Nace, Dallas, Tex.
Norman L. Paul, Lexington, Mass.
Bruce J. Rounsaville, Woodbridge, Conn.

COMMITTEE ON CHILD PSYCHIATRY
Theodore Shapiro, New York, N.Y., Chairperson
James M. Bell, Canaan, N.Y.
Harlow Donald Dunton, New York, N.Y.
Joseph Fischhoff, Detroit, Mich.
John F. McDermott, Jr., Honolulu, Hawaii
John Schowalter, New Haven, Conn.
Peter E. Tanguay, Los Angeles, Calif.
Lenore Terr, San Francisco, Calif.

COMMITTEE ON COLLEGE STUDENTS
Myron B. Liptzin, Chapel Hill, N.C., Chairperson
Robert L. Arnstein, Hamden, Conn.
Varda Backus, La Jolla, Calif.
Harrison P. Eddy, New York, N.Y.
Malkah Tolpin Notman, Brookline, Mass.
Gloria C. Onque, Pittsburgh, Pa.
Elizabeth Aub Reid, Cambridge, Mass.
Earle Silber, Chevy Chase, Md.
Tom G. Stauffer, White Plains, N.Y.

COMMITTEE ON CULTURAL PSYCHIATRY
Ezra E.H. Griffith, New Haven, Conn., Chairperson
Edward F. Foulks, New Orleans, La.
Pedro Ruiz, Houston, Tex.
John P. Spiegel, Waltham, Mass.
Ronald M. Wintrob, Providence, R.I.
Joe Yamamoto, Los Angeles, Calif.

COMMITTEE ON THE FAMILY
W. Robert Beavers, Dallas, Tex., Chairperson
Ellen M. Berman, Merrion, Pa.
Lee Combrinck-Graham, Evanston, Ill.
Ira D. Glick, New York, N.Y.
Frederick Gottlieb, Los Angeles, Calif.
Henry U. Grunebaum, Cambridge, Mass.
Herta A. Guttman, Montreal, Quebec
Judith Landau-Stanton, Rochester, N.Y.
Ann L. Price, Hartford, Conn.
Lyman C. Wynne, Rochester, N.Y.

COMMITTEE ON GOVERNMENTAL AGENCIES
William W. Van Stone, Palo Alto, Calif., Chairperson
James P. Cattell, San Diego, Calif.
Sidney S. Goldensohn, New York, N.Y.
Naomi Heller, Washington, D.C.
Roger Peele, Washington, D.C.
John P. D. Shemo, Charlottesville, Va.

COMMITTEE ON HANDICAPS
Norman R. Bernstein, Cambridge, Mass., Chairperson
Meyer S. Gunther, Wilmette, Ill.
Betty J. Pfefferbaum, Houston, Tex.
William H. Sack, Portland, Oreg.
William A. Sonis, Philadelphia, Pa.
George Tarjan, Los Angeles, Calif.
Thomas G. Webster, Washington, D.C.
Henry H. Work, Bethesda, Md.

COMMITTEE ON HUMAN SEXUALITY
Bertram H. Schaffner, New York, N.Y., Chairperson
Paul L. Adams, Galveston, Tex.
Johanna A. Hoffman, Scottsdale, Ariz.

COMMITTEE ON INTERNATIONAL RELATIONS
Vamik D. Volkan, Charlottesville, Va., Chairperson
Francis F. Barnes, Chevy Chase, Md.
Robert M. Dorn, El Macero, Ca.
John S. Kafka, Washington, D.C.
Otto F. Kernberg, White Plains, N.Y.
John E. Mack, Chestnut Hill, Mass.
Rita R. Rogers, Palos Verdes Estates, Ca.
Stephen B. Shanfield, San Antonio, Tex.

COMMITTEE ON MEDICAL EDUCATION
David R. Hawkins, Chicago, Ill., Chairperson
Gene Abroms, Ardmore, Pa.
Charles M. Culver, Hanover, N.H.
Steven L. Dubovsky, Denver, Colo.
Saul I. Harrison, Torrance, Calif.
Harold I. Lief, Philadelphia, Pa.
Carol Nadelson, Boston, Mass.
Carolyn B. Robinowitz, Washington, D.C.
Stephen C. Scheiber, Deerfield, Ill.
Sidney L. Werkman, Denver, Colo.
Veva H. Zimmerman, New York, N.Y.

COMMITTEE ON MENTAL HEALTH SERVICES
Jose Maria Santiago, Tucson, Ariz., Chairperson
John M. Hamilton, Columbia, Md.
W. Walter Menninger, Topeka, Kans.
Steven S. Sharfstein, Baltimore, Md.
Herzl R. Spiro, Milwaukee, Wis.
William L. Webb, Jr., Hartford, Conn.
George F. Wilson, Somerville, N.J.
Jack A. Wolford, Pittsburgh, Pa.

Committee on Planning and Marketing
Robert W. Gibson, Towson, Md., Chairperson
Allan Beigel, Tucson, Ariz.
Doyle I. Carson, Dallas, Tex.
Robert J. Campbell, New York, N.Y.
Paul J. Fink, Philadelphia, Pa.
Robert S. Garber, Osprey, Fla.
Harvey L. Ruben, New Haven, Conn.
Melvin Sabshin, Washington, D.C.
Michael R. Zales, Quechee, Vt.

Committee on Preventive Psychiatry
Stephen Fleck, New Haven, Conn., Chairperson
Viola W. Bernard, New York, N.Y.
Stanley I. Greenspan, Bethesda, Md.
William H. Hetznecker, Philadelphia, Pa.
Harris B. Peck, New Rochelle, N.Y.
Naomi Rae-Grant, London, Ontario
Morton M. Silverman, Bethesda, Md.
Anne Marie Wolf-Schatz, Conshohocken, Pa.

Committee on Psychiatry and the Community
Kenneth Minkoff, Woburn, Mass., Chairperson
C. Knight Aldrich, Charlottesville, Va.
David G. Greenfield, Guilford, Conn.
H. Richard Lamb, Los Angeles, Calif.
John C. Nemiah, Hanover, N.H.
Rebecca L. Potter, Tucson, Ariz.
Alexander S. Rogawski, Los Angeles, Calif.
John J. Schwab, Louisville, Ky.
John A. Talbott, Baltimore, Md.
Charles B. Wilkinson, Kansas City, Mo.

Committee on Psychiatry and Law
Jonas R. Rappeport, Baltimore, Md., Chairperson
Park E. Dietz, Charlottesville, Va.
John Donnelly, Hartford, Conn.
Carl P. Malmquist, Minneapolis, Minn.
Herbert C. Modlin, Topeka, Kans.
Phillip J. Resnick, Cleveland, Ohio
Loren H. Roth, Pittsburgh, Pa.
Joseph Satten, San Francisco, Calif.
William D. Weitzel, Lexington, Ky.
Howard V. Zonana, New Haven, Conn.

Committee on Psychiatry and Religion
Albert J. Lubin, Woodside, Calif., Chairperson
Sidney Furst, Bronx, N.Y.
Richard C. Lewis, New Haven, Conn.
Earl A. Loomis, Jr., Augusta, Ga.
Abigail R. Ostow, Belmont, Mass.
Mortimer Ostow, Bronx, N.Y.
Sally K. Severino, White Plains, N.Y.
Clyde R. Snyder, Fayetteville, N.C.

Committee on Psychiatry in Industry
Barrie S. Greiff, Newton, Mass., Chairperson
Peter L. Brill, Philadelphia, Pa.
Duane Q. Hagen, St. Louis, Mo.
R. Edward Huffman, Asheville, N.C.
David E. Morrison, Palatine, Ill.
David B. Robbins, Chappaqua, N.Y.
Jay B. Rohrlich, New York, N.Y.
Clarence J. Rowe, St. Paul, Minn.
Jeffrey L. Speller, Alexandria, Va.

Committee on Psychopathology
David A. Adler, Boston, Mass., Chairperson
Jeffrey Berlant, Summit, N.J.
Robert E. Drake, Hanover, N.H.
James M. Ellison, Watertown, Mass.

Howard H. Goldman, Rockville, Md.
Richard E. Renneker, Los Angeles, Calif.

COMMITTEE ON RESEARCH
Robert Cancro, New York, N.Y., Chairperson
Kenneth Z. Altshuler, Dallas, Tex.
Jack A. Grebb, New York, N.Y.
John H. Greist, Madison, Wisc.
Jerry M. Lewis, Dallas, Tex.
Morris A. Lipton, Chapel Hill, N.C.
John G. Looney, Durham, N.C.
Sidney Malitz, New York, N.Y.
Zebulon Taintor, Orangeburg, N.Y.

COMMITTEE ON SOCIAL ISSUES
Ian E. Alger, New York, N.Y., Chairperson
William R. Beardslee, Boston, Mass.
Judith H. Gold, Halifax, Nova Scotia
Roderic Gorney, Los Angeles, Calif.
Martha J. Kirkpatrick, Los Angeles, Calif.
Perry Ottenberg, Philadelphia, Pa.
Kendon W. Smith, Piermont, N.Y.

COMMITTEE ON THERAPEUTIC CARE
Milton Kramer, Cincinnati, Ohio, Chairperson
Bernard Bandler, Cambridge, Mass.
Thomas E. Curtis, Chapel Hill, N.C.
Donald W. Hammersley, Washington, D.C.
William B. Hunter, III, Albuquerque, N.M.
Roberto L. Jimenez, San Antonio, Tex.
William W. Richards, Anchorage, Aka.

COMMITTEE ON THERAPY
Allen D. Rosenblatt, La Jolla, Calif., Chairperson
Jules R. Bemporad, Boston, Mass.
Henry W. Brosin, Tucson, Ariz.
Eugene B. Feigelson, Brooklyn, N.Y.
Robert Michels, New York, N.Y.
Andrew P. Morrison, Cambridge, Mass.
William C. Offenkrantz, Milwaukee, Wis.

CONTRIBUTING MEMBERS
John E. Adams, Gainesville, Fl.
Carlos C. Alden, Jr., Buffalo, N.Y.

Spencer Bayles, Houston, Tex.
C. Christian Beels, New York, N.Y.
Elissa P. Benedek, Ann Arbor, Mich.
Sidney Berman, Washington, D.C.
H. Keith H. Brodie, Durham, N.C.
Charles M. Bryant, San Francisco, Calif.
Ewald W. Busse, Durham, N.C.
Robert N. Butler, New York, N.Y.

Eugene M. Caffey, Jr., Bowie, Md.
Ian L.W. Clancey, Ontario, Canada
Sanford I. Cohen, Boston, Mass.

James S. Eaton, Jr., Washington, D.C.
Lloyd C. Elam, Nashville, Tenn.
Stanley H. Eldred, Belmont, Mass.
Joseph T. English, New York, N.Y.
Louis C. English, Pomona, N.Y.

Sherman C. Feinstein, Highland Park, Ill.
Archie R. Foley, New York, N.Y.
Daniel X. Freedman, Los Angeles, Calif.

Henry J. Gault, Highland Park, Ill.
Alexander Gralnick, Port Chester, N.Y.

Joseph M. Green, Madison, Wis.
Milton Greenblatt, Sylmar, Calif.
Lawrence F. Greenleigh, Los Angeles, Calif.
Jon E. Gudeman, Milwaukee, Wisc.

Stanley Hammons, Lexington, Ky.
J. Cotter Hirschberg, Topeka, Kans.

Jay Katz, New Haven, Conn.
James A. Knight, New Orleans, La.
Othilda M. Krug, Cincinnati, Ohio
Alan I. Levenson, Tucson, Ariz.
Ruth W. Lidz, Woodbridge, Conn.
Orlando B. Lightfoot, Boston, Mass.
Reginald S. Lourie, Chevy Chase, Md.
Norman L. Loux, Sellersville, Pa.

John A. MacLeod, Cincinnati, Ohio
Leo Madow, Philadelphia, Pa.
Charles A. Malone, Cleveland, Ohio
Peter A. Martin, Lake Orion, Mich.
Ake Mattsson, Danderyd, Sweden
Alan A. McLean, Westport, Conn.
David Mendell, Houston, Tex.
Roy W. Menninger, Topeka, Kans.
Mary E. Mercer, Nyack, N.Y.
Derek Miller, Chicago, Ill.
Richard D. Morrill, Boston, Mass.

Joseph D. Noshpitz, Washington, D.C.

Bernard L. Pacella, New York, N.Y.
Herbert Pardes, New York, N.Y.
Marvin E. Perkins, Salem, Va.

David N. Ratnavale, Bethesda, Md.
Kent E. Robinson, Towson, Md.
W. Donald Ross, Cincinnati, Ohio
Lester H. Rudy, Chicago, Ill.
George E. Ruff, Philadelphia, Pa.
David S. Sanders, Los Angeles, Calif.
Donald J. Scherl, Brooklyn, N.Y.
Charles Shagrass, Philadelphia, Pa.
Miles F. Shore, Boston, Mass.
Albert J. Silverman, Ann Arbor, Mich.
Benson R. Snyder, Cambridge, Mass.
David A. Soskis, Bala Cynwyd, Pa.
Jeanne Spurlock, Washington, D.C.
Brandt F. Steele, Denver, Colo.
Alan A. Stone, Cambridge, Mass.
Robert E. Switzer, Dunn Loring, Va.

Perry C. Talkington, Dallas, Tex.
Bryce Templeton, Philadelphia, Pa.
Prescott W. Thompson, Beaverton, Oreg.
Joe P. Tupin, Sacramento, Calif.
John A. Turner, San Francisco, Calif.

Gene L. Usdin, New Orleans, La.

Warren T. Vaughan, Jr., Portola Valley, Calif.

Andrew S. Watson, Ann Arbor, Mich.
Joseph B. Wheelwright, Kentfield, Calif.
Robert L. Williams, Houston, Tex.
Paul Tyler Wilson, Bethesda, Md.
Sherwyn M. Woods, Los Angeles, Calif.

Kent A. Zimmerman, Berkeley, Calif.
Israel Zwerling, Philadelphia, Pa.

LIFE MEMBERS
C. Knight Aldrich, Charlottesville, Va.
Bernard Bandler, Cambridge, Mass.
Walter E. Barton, Hartland, Vt.
Viola W. Bernard, New York, N.Y.
Wilfred Bloomberg, Cambridge, Mass.
Murray Bowen, Chevy Chase, Md.
Henry W. Brosin, Tucson, Ariz.
John Donnelly, Hartford, Conn.
Merrill T. Eaton, Omaha, Neb.
O. Spurgeon English, Narberth, Pa.
Stephen Fleck, New Haven, Conn.
Jerome Frank, Baltimore, Md.
Robert S. Garber, Osprey, Fl.

Robert I. Gibson, Towson, Md.
Paul E. Huston, Iowa City, Iowa
Margaret M. Lawrence, Pomona, N.Y.
Harold I. Lief, Philadelphia, Pa.
Morris A. Lipton, Chapel Hill, N.C.
Judd Marmor, Los Angeles, Calif.
Karl A. Menninger, Topeka, Kans.
Herbert C. Modlin, Topeka, Kans.
John C. Nemiah, Hanover, N.H.
Mabel Ross, Sun City, Ariz.
Julius Schreiber, Washington, D.C.
George Tarjan, Los Angeles, Calif.
Jack A. Wolford, Pittsburgh, Pa.
Henry H. Work, Bethesda, Md.

BOARD OF DIRECTORS

OFFICERS

President
Jerry M. Lewis
Timberlawn Foundation
P.O. Box 270789
Dallas, Tex. 75227

President-Elect
Carolyn B. Robinowitz
Deputy Medical Director
American Psychiatric Association
1400 K Street, N.W.
Washington, D.C. 20005

Secretary
Allan Beigel
30 Camino Español
Tucson, Ariz. 85716

Treasurer
Charles B. Wilkinson
600 E. 22nd Street
Kansas City, Mo. 64108

Board Members
David R. Hawkins
Silvio J. Onesti
John A. Talbott
Lenore Terr

Past Presidents

*William C. Menninger	1946-51
Jack R. Ewalt	1951-53
Walter E. Barton	1953-55
*Sol W. Ginsburg	1955-57
*Dana L. Farnsworth	1957-59
*Marion E. Kenworthy	1959-61
Henry W. Brosin	1961-63
*Leo H. Bartemeier	1963-65
Robert S. Garber	1965-67
Herbert C. Modlin	1967-69
John Donnelly	1969-71
George Tarjan	1971-73
Judd Marmor	1973-75
John C. Nemiah	1975-77
Jack A. Wolford	1977-79
Robert W. Gibson	1979-81
*Jack Weinberg	1981-82
Henry H. Work	1982-85
Michael R. Zales	1985-87

PUBLICATIONS BOARD

Chairman
Alexander S. Rogawski
11665 W. Olympic Blvd. #302
Los Angeles, CA 90064

C. Knight Aldrich
Robert L. Arnstein
Milton Kramer
W. Walter Menninger
Robert A. Solow

Consultant
John C. Nemiah

Ex-Officio
Jerry M. Lewis
Carolyn B. Robinowitz

---

*deceased

CONTRIBUTORS
Abbott Laboratories
American Charitable Fund
Dr. and Mrs. Richard Aron
Mr. Robert C. Baker
Maurice Falk Medical Fund
Mrs. Carol Gold
Grove Foundation, Inc.
Miss Gayle Groves
Ittleson Foundation, Inc.
Mr. Barry Jacobson
Mrs. Allan H. Kalmus
Marion E. Kenworthy—Sarah H. Swift Foundation, Inc.
Mr. Larry Korman
McNeil Pharmaceutical
Phillips Foundation
Sandoz, Inc.
Smith Kline Beckman Corporation
Tappanz Foundation, Inc.
The Upjohn Company
van Amerigen Foundation, Inc.
Wyeth Laboratories
Mr. and Mrs. William A. Zales